Readings in Literary Criticism 12
CRITICS ON WORDSWORTH

CRITICS ON
WORDSWORTH

Readings in Literary Criticism

Edited by Raymond Cowell

Head of the English Department, Nottingham College of Education

London · George Allen and Unwin Ltd

Ruskin House   Museum Street

FIRST PUBLISHED IN 1973

© *George Allen & Unwin Ltd* 1973

ISBN 0 04 801015 4

PRINTED IN GREAT BRITAIN
in 10 *on* 11 *pt Plantin type*
BY CLARKE, DOBLE & BRENDON LIMITED
PLYMOUTH

CONTENTS

INTRODUCTION

Since the early 1800s Wordsworth's influence and status have been so great that the history of his reputation is in many respects the history of changing literary and social tastes in the period. Though he has been criticized and parodied by many, his essential greatness has never been in serious general dispute, compelling recognition, if not always applause, from the vast majority of poets and critics. Of his reputation in his own lifetime, Thomas De Quincey has this to say: 'up to 1820 the name of Wordsworth was trampled under foot; from 1820 to 1830, it was militant; from 1830 to 1835, it has been triumphant'. ('Auto-biography,' *Works*, ed. Masson, II, p. 60). This generalization is not entirely accurate, for *Lyrical Ballads* (1798) received, for the most part, enthusiastic reviews and sold steadily. It was the reception accorded the 1807 *Poems in Two Volumes* which gave Wordsworth his first taste of widespread hostility and incomprehension and led him into a hyper-sensitiveness about his work which some contemporaries interpreted as arrogance and into simplistic theories about the depraved 'public' and the unspoiled 'people' which Patrick Cruttwell analyses so incisively. Francis Jeffrey's maliciously witty campaign against Wordsworth's poetry, begun earlier, found ammunition in these volumes and hurt Wordsworth more than his dismissal of Jeffrey as a dunce and a cox-comb shows. Jeffrey's objections can be seen on analysis to be essentially political, a Whig response to what Hazlitt recognized in his essay on Wordsworth as democratic 'levelling' poetry. This social and political basis of Wordsworth's revolution is examined by Christopher Wordsworth and T. S. Eliot too, though its full implications are perhaps not yet fully recognized. Between 1807 and the early 1820s, when collected editions of his work began to appear, Wordsworth's reputation was indeed 'trampled under foot', even, in many cases, by contemporary poets who at best had mixed feelings about his work.

But mixed feelings are preferable, I think, to the uncritical 'Words-worthianism' of some Victorian protagonists of Wordsworth's poetry. A great deal of early Victorian comment—by J. S. Mill and Walter Bage-hot, for example—is in many ways sensible, though showing traces of proselytizing fervour, but by 1879 Matthew Arnold's attack on the Wordsworthians was overdue. In his bid to save Wordsworth from the Wordsworthians Arnold asserted that their uncritical acceptance of the whole of Wordsworth as almost Holy Writ and their extraction from his writings of a cosily reassuring 'philosophy' did his poetry a dis-service and he urged a closer concern with the poetry as poetry—parti-cularly that contained in his own selection!

Though Macaulay for one dismissed *The Prelude* as an irrelevance when it was posthumously published in 1850, and though its central place within the Wordsworth canon has been recognized only in this century, its appearance did intensify what now appears to be endless speculation about the causes of Wordsworth's decline. Of course 'Tintern Abbey' and the 'Immortality Ode' had given some basis for such speculation but the self-searching of *The Prelude* released a flood of theories and of biographical research which only rarely illuminated the work itself. Theories about the reasons for Wordsworth's undeniable decline require as a basis more convincing theories about the sources of his greatness than we yet have, and it is salutary to remember that in a letter of 1843 Wordsworth said with unashamed candour: 'no change has taken place in my manner for the last forty-five years'. Such a statement measures the gulf between the constant experimentalism of our own century and the more stable and traditional assumptions of even a revolutionary like Wordsworth. The essential, and simple, points about the later Wordsworth were made by William Minto in 1889, though several of the modern critics represented in this selection have illuminating incidental things to say about the causes of the decline.

Another recurrent, and not always fruitful, theme of Wordsworthian criticism has been the allegation or rebuttal of political apostasy. Recently such criticism has given way to an attempt to see Wordsworth's relation to his times in rather more complex terms than the traditional view of the young revolutionary declining into the old reactionary permits, and the work of Piper, for example, goes some way towards representing the milieu out of which Wordsworth's early poetry grew. Huxley, in 1929, made the allegation of poetic apostasy, and it is certainly worth bearing in mind the strictures made by Huxley and Madariaga in their attempts to prove the insularity of Wordsworth. The English tradition of modern Wordsworth criticism, stemming from the essentially academic intelligences of Bradley and Garrod, sometimes lacks the astringency and discrimination represented by Huxley and Madariaga.

Wordsworth's avowed aspirations to write a philosophical epic, *The Recluse*, have encouraged philosophers to treat his poetry as a series of philosophical statements and, not surprisingly, they have often concluded that Wordsworth's philosophy is neither original nor coherent. More interestingly, several literary critics have explored his place in the history of literary ideas without losing sight of the actual poetry, so that the nature of the Wordsworthian Imagination has been illuminated in the studies of, for example, Willey, Hartman and Prickett. These critics agree in detecting in Wordsworth's concept of the Imagination certain difficulties and contradictions but also recognize that in a sense his poetry's greatness arises from these characteristics.

If all this suggests that Wordsworth is accessible only by arduous and circuitous routes, the sensitive and subtle analyses of individual poems by Bloom, Gérard and Danby, using only the now familiar tools of 'practical criticism', show that this is not the case. Even the more ambitious poems, like *The Prelude*, need not inspire gratuitous erudition, as Edwin Morgan shows in his demonstration of the innate poetic difficulties of an autobiographical epic, and of the triumphs of Wordsworth's method. Similarly, Professor King, in emphasizing the universality of what is often seen as an intensely private and personal poem, shows that the 'Immortality Ode' is at once simpler and more profound than some ingenious critics have made it seem.

Any selection from the vast mass of Wordsworthian criticism and scholarship must seem arbitrary. Clearly Professor Moorman's biography does not lend itself to brief quotation, nor does Jonathan Wordsworth's recent study of the MSS of 'The Ruined Cottage'. What is clear is that Wordsworth's poetry still presents a critical challenge and that much remains to be done in defining and elucidating, for example, the nature of his originality and the extent of his influence. The last, characteristically bold, word should be with Wordsworth who in 1815 gave what is perhaps the basic reason for the mass and wealth of Wordsworth criticism: 'Genius is the introduction of a new element into the intellectual universe.'

Nottingham, 1972   Raymond Cowell

ACKNOWLEDGEMENTS

We are grateful to the following for permission to use copyright material from the works whose titles follow in brackets:

Macmillan, London and Basingstoke (A. C. Bradley's *Oxford Lectures on Poetry*, 'Wordsworth'); Clarendon Press, Oxford (H. W. Garrod's *Wordsworth: Lectures and Essays*); Constable (Salvador de Madariaga's *Shelley and Calderon and Other Essays on English and Spanish Poetry*, 'The Case of Wordsworth'); Mrs Laura Huxley and Chatto and Windus (Aldous Huxley's *Do What You Will*, 'Wordsworth in the Tropic's'); Faber and Faber Ltd (T. S. Eliot's *The Use of Poetry and The Use of Criticism*; 'Wordsworth and Coleridge'); Chatto and Windus Ltd (Basil Willey's 'Postscript: On Wordsworth and the Locke Tradition' from *The Seventeenth Century Background*); The University of the South (Patrick Cruttwell's 'Wordsworth, the Public and the People' from Vol. LXIV, 1956, of *The Sewanee Review*); University of London, Athlone Press (H. V. Piper's *The Active Universe: Pantheism and the Concept of Imagination in the English Romantic Poets*, 1962); Faber and Faber Ltd (Harold Bloom's *The Visionary Company*: 'William Wordsworth: 4. Natural Man'); Boston University (A. S. Gérard's 'Dark Passages: Exploring "Tintern Abbey"' from *Studies in Romanticism*, Vol. III); Routledge and Kegan Paul Ltd (John Danby's *The Simple Wordsworth*: 'Irony in *Simon Lee*'); F. W. Bateson (Edwin Morgan's 'A Prelude to *The Prelude*' from *Essays in Criticism* V, 1955); Yale University Press (Geoffrey H. Hartman's *Wordsworth's Poetry 1787–1814*. Copyright © 1964 by Yale University); University of London, Athlone Press (A. King's *Wordsworth and the Artist's Vision*: 'The Two Childhoods in the "Immortality Ode"'); Cambridge University Press (Stephen Prickett's *Coleridge and Wordsworth: The Poetry of Growth*. © Cambridge University Press 1970).

Early Critics on Wordsworth 1798-1930

ROBERT SOUTHEY (1774-1843)

With pleasure we turn to the serious pieces, the better part of the volume. *The Foster Mother's Tale* is in the best style of dramatic narrative. *The Dungeon*, and the *Lines upon the Yew Tree Seat*, are beautiful. *The Tale of the Female Vagrant* is written in the stanza, not the style, of Spenser. . . . Admirable as this poem is, the author seems to discover still superior powers in the *Lines written near Tintern Abbey*. On reading this production, it is impossible not to lament that he should have condescended to write such pieces as the *Last of the Flock, the Convict*, and most of the ballads. In the whole range of English poetry, we scarcely recollect anything superior to a part of the following passage:

> 'And so I dare to hope,
> Though changed, no doubt, from what I was when first
> I came among these hills.' etc.

The 'experiment', we think, has failed, not because the language of conversation is little adapted to 'the purposes of poetic pleasure', but because it has been tried upon uninteresting subjects. Yet every piece discovers genius; and, ill as the author has frequently employed his talents, they certainly rank him with the best of living poets.

From a review of *Lyrical Ballads, The Critical Review*, XXIV, October 1798, pp. 197–204. Extracts from this review are reprinted in: *Lyrical Ballads* edited by R. L. Brett and A. R. Jones, London: Methuen, 1963, pp. 313–15 (314), hereafter *Brett and Jones*. (The page numbers before the bracket give the beginning and end of the whole article, those within the bracket the pages of the actual extract.)

DR CHARLES BURNEY (1757-1817)

The Convict. What a description! What misplaced commiseration! . . . We do not comprehend the drift of lavishing that tenderness and compassion on a criminal, which should be reserved for virtue in unmerited misery and distress, suffering untimely death from accident, injustice, or disease.

Lines written near Tintern Abbey. The reflections of no common mind; poetical, beautiful, and philosophical: but somewhat tinctured with gloomy, narrow, and unsociable ideas of seclusion from the commerce of the world: as if men were born to live in woods and wilds, unconnected with each other. . . . So much genius and originality are discovered in this publication, that we wish to see another from the same hand, written on more elevated subjects and in a more cheerful disposition.

From a review of *Lyrical Ballads*, *The Monthly Review*, XXIX, June 1799, pp. 202–10. See *Brett and Jones*, pp. 315–17 (317).

REVEREND FRANCIS WRANGHAM (?) (1769-1842)

Whatever may be thought of these poems, it is evident that they are not to be confounded with the flood of poetry which is poured forth in such profusion by the modern Bards of Science, or their Brethren, the Bards of Insipidity. The author has thought for himself; he has deeply studied human nature, in the book of human action; and he has adopted his language from the same sources as his feelings. Aware that his Poems are so materially different from those upon which general approbation is at present bestowed, he has now defended them in a Preface of some length; not with the foolish hope of reasoning his readers into the approbation of these particular Poems, but as a necessary justification of the species of poetry to which they belong. This Preface, though written in some parts with a degree of metaphysical obscurity, conveys much penetrating judicious observation, important at all times, but especially when, as it is well observed, 'the invaluable works of our elder writers are driven into neglect by frantic novels, sickly and stupid German tragedies, and deluges of idle and extravagant stories in verse'. Perhaps it would be expecting too much from any one but Shakespeare, were we to demand that he should be the Poet of human nature. It would be no mean, it would indeed be a very lofty praise, to assert of a writer, that he is able to pour into other bosoms powerful feelings of a particular class, or belonging to a particular order of men. To this praise, Mr Wordsworth lays a well-supported claim. He declares himself the poet chiefly of low and rustic life (some specimens of ability he has given in other lines, but this is evidently his excellence) and he pourtrays it, not under its disgusting forms, but in situations affording, as he thinks, the best soil for the essential passions of the heart, incorporated with an elementary and durable state of manners, and with the beautiful and permanent forms of nature.[1]

[1] Mr Wordsworth seems to be peculiarly well situated for the subjects of such a study. The vicinity of the Lakes in Cumberland and Westmorland (the scene

From a review of the second edition of *Lyrical Ballads*, *The British Critic*, XVII, February 1801, pp. 125–31. See *Brett and Jones*, pp. 320–5 (321–2). The attribution of this unsigned review to Wrangham is queried by John O. Hayden, *The Romantic Reviewers: 1802–1824*, London: Routledge and Kegan Paul, 1969, p. 79n.

JOHN WILSON (the 'Christopher North' of Blackwood's Magazine) (1785-1854)

To you, sir, mankind are indebted for a species of poetry, which will continue to afford pleasure while respect is paid to virtuous feelings, and while sensibility continues to pour forth tears of rapture. The flimsy ornaments of language, used to conceal meanness of thought and want of feeling, may for a short time captivate the ignorant and unwary; but true taste will discover the imposture, and expose the authors of it to merited contempt. The real feelings of human nature, expressed in simple and forcible language, will, on the contrary, please those only who are capable of entertaining them, and in proportion of the attention which we pay to the faithful delineation of such feelings, will be the enjoyment derived from them. The poetry, therefore, which is the language of Nature, is certain of immortality, provided circumstances do not occur to pervert the feelings of humanity, and occasion a complete revolution in the government of the mind. . . .

They represent the enjoyment resulting from the cultivation of the social affections of our nature; they inculcate a conscientious regard to the rights of our fellow-men; they show that every creature on the face of the earth is entitled in some measure to our kindness. They prove that in every mind, however depraved, there exist some qualities deserving our esteem. They point out the proper way to happiness. They show that such a thing as perfect misery does not exist. They flash on our souls convictions of immortality. Considered, therefore, in this view, the *Lyrical Ballads* is, to use your own words, the book which I value next to my Bible; and though I may, perhaps, never have the happiness of seeing you, yet I always consider you as a friend, who has, by his instructions, done me a service which it can never be in my power to repay. Your instructions have afforded me inexpressible pleasure; it will be my own fault if I do not reap from them much advantage.

From a letter to Wordsworth by the seventeen-year-old Wilson, May 1802. See *Brett and Jones*, pp. 325–30 (325–6, 327–8).

of most of his Poems) is chiefly inhabited by an order of men nearly extinct in other parts of England. These are small farmers, called in that part of the country 'Statesmen', who, cultivating their own little property, are raised above the immediate pressure of want, with very few opportunities of acquiring wealth. They are a mild, hospitable people, with some turn for reading; and their personal appearance is, for the most part, interesting.

FRANCIS JEFFREY (1773-1850)

(i)

It has been argued, indeed, (for men will argue in support of what they do not venture to practise,) that, as the middling and lower orders of society constitute by far the greater part of mankind, so their feelings and expressions should interest more extensively, and may be taken, more fairly than any other, for the standards of what is natural and true. To this it seems obvious to answer, that the arts that aim at exciting admiration and delight, do not take their models from what is ordinary, but from what is excellent; and that our interest in the representation of any event does not depend upon our familiarity with the original, but on its intrinsic importance, and the celebrity of the parties it concerns. The sculptor employs his art in delineating the graces of Antinous or Apollo, and not in the representation of those ordinary forms that belong to the crowd of his admirers. When a chieftain perishes in battle, his followers mourn more for him than for thousands of their equals that may have fallen around him. . . .

In making these strictures on the perverted taste for simplicity, that seems to distinguish our modern school of poetry, we have no particular allusion to Mr Southey, or the production now before us: On the contrary, he appears to us to be less addicted to this fault than most of his fraternity; and if we were in want of examples to illustrate the preceding observations, we should certainly look for them in the effusions of that poet who commemorates with so much effect, the chattering of Harry Gill's teeth, tells the tale of the one-eyed huntsman, 'who had a cheek like a cherry', and beautifully warns his studious friend of the risk he ran of 'growing double'. . . .

Our new school of poetry has a moral character also; though it may not be possible, perhaps, to delineate it quite so concisely.

A splenetic and idle discontent with the existing institutions of society, seems to be at the bottom of all their serious and peculiar sentiments. Instead of contemplating the wonders and pleasures which civilization has created for mankind, they are perpetually brooding over the disorders by which its progress has been attended. They are filled with horror and compassion at the sight of poor men spending their blood in the quarrels of princes, and brutifying their sublime capabilities in the drudgery of unremitting labour. For all sorts of vice in the lower orders of society they have the same virtuous horror, and the same tender compassion. While the existence of these offences overpowers them with grief and confusion, they never permit themselves to feel the smallest indignation or dislike towards the offenders. The present vicious constitution of society alone is responsible for all these enormities; the poor sinners are but the helpless victims or instruments of its disorders, and could not possibly have avoided the errors into which they have been betrayed. Though they can bear with crimes, therefore, they cannot reconcile themselves to punishments; and have an unconquerable antipathy to prisons, gibbets, and houses of correction, as engines of oppression, and instruments of atrocious injustice. While the plea of moral necessity is thus artfully brought forward to convert all the excesses of the poor into innocent misfortunes, no sort of indulgence is shown to the offences of the powerful and rich. Their oppressions, and seductions, and debaucheries, are the theme of many an angry verse; and the indignation and abhorrence of the readers is relentlessly conjured up against those perturbators of society and scourges of mankind.

(ii)

With Mr Wordsworth and his friends, it is plain that their peculiarities of diction are things of choice, and not of accident. They write as they do, upon principle and system; and it evidently costs them much pains to keep *down* to the standard which they have proposed to themselves. They are, to the full, as much mannerists, too, as the poetasters who ring changes on the commonplaces of magazines versification; and all the difference between them is, that they borrow their phrases from a different and scantier *gradus ad Parnassum*. If they were, indeed, to discard all imitation and set phraseology, and to bring in no words merely for show or for metre—as much, perhaps, might be gained in freedom and originality, as would infallibly be lost in allusion and authority; but, in point of fact, the new poets are just as great borrowers as the old; only that, instead of borrowing from the more popular passages of their illustrious predecessors, they have preferred furnishing themselves from vulgar ballads and plebeian nurseries.

(iii)

Long habits of seclusion, and an excessive ambition of originality, can alone account for the disproportion which seems to exist between this author's taste and his genius; or for the devotion with which he has sacrificed so many precious gifts at the shrine of those paltry idols which he has set up for himself among his lakes and his mountains. Solitary musings, amidst such scenes, might no doubt be expected to nurse up the mind to the majesty of poetical conception (though it is remarkable, that all the greater poets lived, or had lived, in the full current of society), but the collision of equal minds—the admonition of prevailing impressions—seems necessary to reduce its redundancies, and repress that tendency to extravagance or puerility, into which the self-indulgence and self-admiration of genius is so apt to be betrayed, when it is allowed to wanton, without awe or restraint, in the triumph and delight of its own intoxication. That its flights should be graceful and glorious in the eyes of men, it seems almost to be necessary that they should be made in the consciousness that men's eyes are to behold them,—and that the inward transport and vigour by which they are inspired, should be tempered by an occasional reference to what will be thought of them by those ultimate dispensers of glory. An habitual and

B

general knowledge of the few settled and permanent maxims, which form the canon of general taste in all large and polished societies—a certain tact, which informs us at once that many things, which we still love and are moved by in secret, must necessarily be despised as childish, or derided as absurd, in all such societies—though it will not stand in the place of genius, seems necessary to the success of its exertions; and though it will never enable anyone to produce the higher beauties of art, can alone secure the talent which does produce them, from errors that must render it useless. Those who have most of the talent, however, commonly acquire this knowledge with the greatest facility; and if Mr Wordsworth, instead of confining himself almost entirely to the society of the dalesmen and cottagers and little children, who form the subjects of his book, had condescended to mingle a little more with the people that were to read and judge of it, we cannot help thinking that its texture might have been considerably improved: at least it appears to us to be absolutely impossible, that anyone who had lived or mixed familiarly with men of literature and ordinary judgement in poetry, (of course we exclude the coadjutors and disciples of his own school) could ever have fallen into such gross faults, or so long mistaken them for beauties. His first essays we looked upon in a good degree as poetical paradoxes—maintained experimentally, in order to display talent, and court notoriety;—and so maintained, with no more serious belief in their truth, than is usually generated by an ingenious and animated defence of other paradoxes. But when we find that he has been for twenty years exclusively employed upon articles of this very fabric, and that he has still enough of raw material on hand to keep him so employed for twenty years to come, we cannot refuse him the justice of believing that he is a sincere convert to his own system, and must ascribe the peculiarities of his composition, not to any transient affectation, or accidental caprice of imagination, but to a settled perversity of taste or understanding, which has been fostered, if not altogether created, by the circumstances to which we have already alluded.

(i) From a review of Southey's *Thalaba*, *The Edinburgh Review*, I, October 1802, pp. 63–83. See *Romantic Perspectives*, edited by Patricia Hodgart and Theodore Redpath, London: Harrap, 1964, pp. 168–70, hereafter *Hodgart and Redpath*.
(ii) From a review of *Poems in Two Volumes*, *The Edinburgh Review*, XI, October 1807, pp. 214–31. See *Hodgart and Redpath*, pp. 179–80.
(iii) From a review of *The Excursion*, *The Edinburgh Review*, XXIV, November 1814, pp. 1–30. See *Hodgart and Redpath*, pp. 186–8.

WILLIAM WORDSWORTH

Never forget what I believe was observed to you by Coleridge, that every great and original writer, in proportion as he is great or original, must

himself create the taste by which he is to be relished; he must teach the
art by which he is to be seen; this, in a certain degree, even to all
persons, however wise and pure may be their lives, and however un-
vitiated their taste; but for those who dip into books in order to give an
opinion of them, or talk about them to take up an opinion—for this
multitude of unhappy, and misguided, and misguiding beings, an entire
regeneration must be produced; and if this be possible, it must be a work
of time. To conclude, my ears are stone-dead to this idle buzz, and my
flesh as insensible as iron to these petty stings; and after what I have said
I am sure yours will be the same. I doubt not that you will share with me
an invincible confidence that my writings (and among them these little
Poems) will co-operate with the benign tendencies in human nature and
society, wherever found; and that they will, in their degree, be efficacious in making men wiser, better and happier.

From a letter to Lady Beaumont of 21 May 1807. *The Letters of
William and Dorothy Wordsworth. The Middle Years,* 2 vols, edited by
Ernest de Selincourt, Oxford: Clarendon Press, 1937, I, pp. 125-31
(130-1).

HENRY CRABB ROBINSON (1775-1867)

But on my gently alluding to the lines: 'Three feet long and two
feet wide', and confessing that I dare not read them out in company,
he said, 'they ought to be liked'.

From an entry in his diary for 9 May 1815. *The Diary of Henry Crabb
Robinson,* an abridgement edited with an introduction by Derek
Hudson, London: Oxford University Press, 1967, p. 40.

PERCY BYSSHE SHELLEY (1792-1822)

(i)

Poet of Nature, thou hast wept to know
   That things depart which never may return:
Childhood and youth, friendship, and love's first glow,
   Have fled like sweet dreams, leaving them to mourn.
These common woes I feel. One loss is mine,
   Which thou too feel'st, yet I alone deplore.
Thou wert as a lone star whose light did shine
   On some frail bark in winter's midnight roar:
Thou hast like to a rock-built refuge stood
Above the blind and battling multitude:

In honoured poverty thy voice did weave
  Songs consecrate to truth and liberty.
Deserting these, thou leavest me to grieve,
  Thus, having been, that thou shouldst cease to be.

(ii)

A printer's boy, folding those pages,
  Fell slumbrously upon one side,
Like those famed Seven who slept three ages.
To wakeful frenzy's vigil-rages,
  As opiates, were the same applied.

Even the Reviewers who were hired
  To do the work of his reviewing,
With adamantine nerves, grew tired;—
Gaping and torpid they retired,
  To dream of what they should be doing.

And worse and worse, the drowsy curse
  Yawned in him till it grew a pest;
A wide contagious atmosphere
Creeping like cold though all things near;
  A power to infect and to infest.

His servant-maids and dogs grew dull;
  His kitten, late a sportive elf;
The woods and lakes so beautiful,
Of dim stupidity were full;
  All grew dull as Peter's self.

The earth under his feet, the springs
  Which lived within it a quick life—
The air, the winds of many wings
That fan it with new murmurings—
  Were dead to their harmonious strife.

The birds and beasts within the wood,
  The insects and each creeping thing,
Were now a silent multitude;
Love's work was left unwrought—no brood
  Near Peter's house took wing.

And every neighbouring cottager
  Stupidly yawned upon the other;
No jackass brayed, no little cur
Cocked up his ears; no man would stir
  To save a dying mother.

Yet all from that charmed district went
  But some half-idiot and half-knave,

Who, rather than pay any rent,
Would live with marvellous content
  Over his father's grave.

No bailiff dared within that space,
  For fear of the dull charm, to enter;
A man would bear upon his face,
For fifteen months, in any case,
  The yawn of such a venture.

Seven miles above—below—around—
  This pest of dulness holds its sway;
A ghastly life without a sound;
To Peter's soul the spell is bound—
  How should it ever pass away?

(i) 'To Wordsworth' (1816), *The Complete Poetical Works of Percy
Bysshe Shelley*, edited by Thora Hutchinson, Oxford: University
Press, 1907, p. 522.
(ii) Conclusion of 'Peter Bell the Third' (1819), satirizing *Peter Bell*
of that year, ibid., p. 357.

JOHN KEATS (1795-1821)

I will return to Wordsworth—whether or no he has an extended vision
or a circumscribed grandeur—whether he is an eagle in his nest, or
on the wing—And to be more explicit and to show you how tall I stand
by the giant, I will put down a simile of human life as far as I now
perceive it; that is, to the point to which I say we both have arrived at—
Well—I compare human life to a large Mansion of Many Apartments,
two of which I can only describe, the doors of the rest being as yet shut
upon me—The first we step into we call the infant or thoughtless Chamber, in which we remain as long as we do not think—We remain there a
long while, and notwithstanding the doors of the second Chamber
remain wide open, showing a bright appearance, we care not to hasten
to it; but are at length imperceptibly impelled by the awakening of the
thinking principle—within us—we no sooner get into the second
Chamber, which I shall call the Chamber of Maiden-Thought, than we
become intoxicated with the light and the atmosphere, we see nothing
but pleasant wonders, and think of delaying there for ever in delight:
However among the effects this breathing is father of is that tremendous
one of sharpening one's vision into the [head/heart] and nature of
Man—of convincing ones nerves that the World is full of Misery and
Heartbreak, Pain, Sickness and oppression—whereby This Chamber of
Maiden Thought becomes gradually darken'd and at the same time on
all sides of it many doors are set open—but all dark—all leading to dark

passages—We see not the ballance of good and evil. We are in a Mist—
We are now in that state—We feel the 'burden of the Mystery', To this
point was Wordsworth come, as far as I can conceive when he wrote
'Tintern Abbey' and it seems to me that his Genius is explorative of
those dark Passages. Now if we live, and go on thinking, we too shall
explore them. he is a Genius and superior [to] us, in so far as he can,
more than we, make discoveries, and shed a light in them—Here I must
think Wordsworth is deeper than Milton—though I think it has depen-
ded more upon the general and gregarious advance of intellect, than individual greatness of Mind—From the Paradise Lost and the other
Works of Milton, I hope it is not too presuming, even between ourselves
to say, his Philosophy, human and divine, may be tolerably understood
by one not much advanced in years, In his time englishmen were just
emancipated from a great superstition—and Men had got hold of certain
points and resting places in reasoning which were too newly born to be
doubted, and too much [opposed/oppressed] by the Mass of Europe not
to be thought etherial and authentically divine—who could gainsay his
ideas on virtue, vice, and Chastity in Comus, just at the time of the dismissal of Cod-pieces and a hundred other disgraces? who would not
rest satisfied with his hintings at good and evil in the Paradise Lost,
when just free from the inquisition and burrning in Smithfield? The
Reformation produced such immediate and great[s] benefits, that
Protestantism was considered under the immediate eye of heaven, and
its own remaining Dogmas and superstitions, then, as it were, regener-
ated, constituted those resting places and seeming sure points of
Reasoning—from that I have mentioned, Milton, whatever he may have
thought in the sequel, appears to have been content with these by his
writings—He did not think into the human heart, as Wordsworth has
done—Yet Milton as a Philosop[h]er, had sure as great powers as
Wordsworth—What is then to be inferr'd? O many things—It proves
there is really a grand march of intellect—, It proves that a mighty
providence subdues the mightiest Minds to the service of the time being,
whether it be in human Knowledge or Religion.

From a letter of 3 May 1818 to John Hamilton Reynolds. *The Letters
of John Keats*, edited by Hyder Edward Rollins, 2 vols., Cambridge
University Press, 1958, I, pp. 275–83 (280–2).
(See the article by Albert Gérard for a development of Keats's
remarks.)

SAMUEL TAYLOR COLERIDGE (1772-1834)

The second defect I can generalize with tolerable accuracy, if the reader
will pardon an uncouth and new-coined word. There is, I should say,
not seldom a *matter-of-factness* in certain poems. This may be divided
into, *first*, a laborious minuteness and fidelity in the representation of

objects, and their positions, as they appeared to the poet himself; *secondly*, the insertion of accidental circumstances, in order to the full explanation of his living characters, their dispositions and actions; which circumstances might be necessary to establish the probability of a statement in real life, where nothing is taken for granted by the hearer, but appear superfluous in poetry, where the reader is willing to believe for his own sake.

> From Chapter XXII of *Biographia Literaria* (1817), edited by George Watson (Everyman's Library), London: Dent, 1956, p. 251.
> (See the extract from Stephen Prickett's book for a development of this Coleridgean attitude.)

THOMAS LOVE PEACOCK (1785-1866)

A poet in our time is a semi-barbarian in a civilized community. He lives in the days that are past. His ideas, thoughts, feelings, associations, are all with barbarous manners, obsolete customs, and exploded super-stitions. The march of his intellect is like that of a crab, backward. The brighter the light diffused around him by the progress of reason, the thicker is the darkness of antiquated barbarism, in which he buries him-self like a mole, to throw up the barren hillocks of his Cimmerian labours. The philosophic mental tranquillity which looks round with an equal eye on all external things, collects a store of ideas, discriminates their relative value, assigns to all their proper place, and from the materials of useful knowledge thus collected, appreciated, and arranged, forms new combinations that impress the stamp of their power and utility on the real business of life, is diametrically the reverse of that frame of mind which poetry inspires, or from which poetry can emanate. The highest inspirations of poetry are resolvable into three ingredients: the rant of unregulated passion, the whining of exaggerated feeling, and the cant of factitious sentiment: and can therefore serve only to ripen a splendid lunatic like Alexander, a puling driveller like Werter, or a morbid dreamer like Wordsworth.

> From 'The Four Ages of Poetry (1820), *Memoirs of Shelley and Other Essays and Reviews*, edited by Howard Mills, London: Rupert Hart-Davis, 1970, pp. 129-30.

WILLIAM HAZLITT (1778-1830)

In a word, his poetry is founded on setting up an opposition (and pushing it to the utmost length) between the natural and the artificial; between the spirit of humanity, and the spirit of fashion and of the world!

It is one of the innovations of the time. It partakes of, and is carried along with, the revolutionary movement of our age: the political changes of the day were the model on which he formed and conducted his poetical experiments. His Muse (it cannot be denied, and without this we cannot explain its character at all) is a levelling one. It proceeds on a principle of equality, and strives to reduce all things to the same standard. It is distinguished by a proud humility. It relies upon its own resources, and disdains external show and relief. It takes the commonest events and objects, as a test to prove that nature is always interesting from its inherent truth and beauty, without any of the ornaments of dress or pomp of circumstances to set it off. Hence the unaccountable mixture of seeming simplicity and real abstruseness in the *Lyrical Ballads*. Fools have laughed at, wise men scarcely understand them. He takes a subject or a story merely as pegs or loops to hang thought and feeling on; the incidents are trifling, in proportion to his contempt for imposing appearances; the reflections are profound, according to the gravity and the aspiring pretensions of his mind.

His popular, inartificial style gets rid (at a blow) of all the trappings of verse, of all the high places of poetry: 'the cloud-capt towers, the solemn temples, the gorgeous palaces', are swept to the ground, and 'like the baseless fabric of a vision, leave not a wreck behind'. All the traditions of learning, all the superstitions of age, are obliterated and effaced. We begin *de novo*, on a *tabula rasa* of poetry. The purple pall, the nodding plume of tragedy are exploded as mere pantomime and trick, to return to the simplicity of truth and nature. Kings, queens, priests, nobles, the altar and the throne, the distinctions of rank, birth, wealth, power, 'the judge's robe, the marshal's truncheon, the ceremony that to great ones 'longs', are not to be found here. The author tramples on the pride of art with greater pride. The Ode and Epode, the Strophe and the Antistrophe, he laughs to scorn. The harp of Homer, the trump of Pindar and of Alcæus are still. The decencies of costume, the decorations of vanity are stripped off without mercy as barbarous, idle, and Gothic. The jewels in the crisped hair, the diadem on the polished brow are thought meretricious, theatrical, vulgar; and nothing contents his fastidious taste beyond a simple garland of flowers. Neither does he avail himself of the advantages which nature or accident holds out to him. He chooses to have his subject a foil to his invention, to owe nothing but to himself. He gathers manna in the wilderness, he strikes the barren rock for the gushing moisture. He elevates the mean by the strength of his own aspirations; he clothes the naked with beauty and grandeur from the stores of his own recollections. No cypress grove loads his verse with funeral pomp: but his imagination lends 'a sense of joy

To the bare trees and mountains bare,
And grass in the green field.'

No storm, no shipwreck startles us by its horrors: but the rainbow lifts its head in the cloud, and the breeze sighs through the withered fern.

No sad vicissitude of fate, no overwhelming catastrophe in nature
deforms his page: but the dew-drop glitters on the bending flower, the
tear collects in the glistening eye.

> 'Beneath the hills, along the flowery vales,
> The generations are prepared; the pangs,
> The internal pangs are ready; the dread strife
> Of poor humanity's afflicted will,
> Struggling in vain with ruthless destiny.'

As the lark ascends from its low bed on fluttering wing, and salutes the
morning skies; so Mr Wordsworth's unpretending Muse, in russet
guise, scales the summits of reflection, while it makes the round earth
its footstool, and its home!

Possibly a good deal of this may be regarded as the effect of disappointed views and an inverted ambition. Prevented by native pride
and indolence from climbing the ascent of learning or greatness, taught
by political opinions to say to the vain pomp and glory of the world,
'I hate ye', seeing the path of classical and artificial poetry blocked up
by the cumbrous ornaments of style and turgid *commonplaces*, so that
nothing more could be achieved in that direction but by the most
ridiculous bombast or the tamest servility; he has turned back partly
from the bias of his mind, partly perhaps from a judicious policy—has
struck into the sequestered vale of humble life, sought out the Muse
among sheep-cotes and hamlets and the peasant's mountain-haunts, has
discarded all the tinsel pageantry of verse, and endeavoured (not in
vain) to aggrandise the trivial and add the charm of novelty to the
familiar. No one has shown the same imagination in raising trifles into
importance: no one has displayed the same pathos in treating of the
simplest feelings of the heart. Reserved, yet haughty, having no unruly
or violent passions, (or those passions having been early suppressed,)
Mr Wordsworth has passed his life in solitary musing, or in daily
converse with the face of nature. He exemplifies in an eminent degree
the power of *association*; for his poetry has no other source or character.
He has dwelt among pastoral scenes, till each object has become connected with a thousand feelings, a link in the chain of thought, a fibre
of his own heart. Every one is by habit and familiarity strongly attached
to the place of his birth, or to objects that recall the most pleasing and
eventful circumstances of his life. But to the author of the *Lyrical
Ballads*, nature is a kind of home; and he may be said to take a personal
interest in the universe. There is no image so insignificant that it has
not in some mood or other found the way into his heart: no sound that
does not awaken the memory of other years.—

> 'To him the meanest flower that blows can give
> Thoughts that do often lie too deep for tears.'

The daisy looks up to him with sparkling eye as an old acquaintance:
the cuckoo haunts him with sounds of early youth not to be expressed: a

linnet's nest startles him with boyish delight: an old withered thorn is weighed down with a heap of recollections: a grey cloak, seen on some wild moor, torn by the wind, or drenched in the rain, afterwards becomes an object of imagination to him: even the lichens on the rock have a life and being in his thoughts. He has described all these objects in a way and with an intensity of feeling that no one else had done before him, and has given a new view or aspect of nature. He is in this sense the most original poet now living, and the one whose writings could the least be spared: for they have no substitute elsewhere. The vulgar do not read them, the learned, who see all things through books, do not understand them, the great despise, the fashionable may ridicule them: but the author has created himself an interest in the heart of the retired and lonely student of nature, which can never die. Persons of this class will still continue to feel what he has felt: he has expressed what they might in vain wish to express, except with glistening eye and faultering tongue! There is a lofty philosophic tone, a thoughtful humanity, infused into his pastoral vein. Remote from the passions and events of the great world, he has communicated interest and dignity to the primal movements of the heart of man, and ingrafted his own conscious reflections on the casual thoughts of hinds and shepherds. Nursed amidst the grandeur of mountain scenery, he has stooped to have a nearer view of the daisy under his feet, or plucked a branch of white-thorn from the spray: but in describing it, his mind seems imbued with the majesty and solemnity of the objects around him—the tall rock lifts its head in the erectness of his spirit; the cataract roars in the sound of his verse; and in its dim and mysterious meaning, the mists seem to gather in the hollows of Helvellyn, and the forked Skiddaw hovers in the distance. There is little mention of mountainous scenery in Mr Wordsworth's poetry; but by internal evidence one might be almost sure that it was written in a mountainous country, from its bareness, its simplicity, its loftiness and its depth!

From 'Mr Wordsworth', *The Spirit of the Age* (1825), *The Complete Works*, edited by P. P. Howe, XI, pp. 86–95 (87–90).

WILLIAM BLAKE (1757-1827)

I see in Wordsworth the Natural Man rising up against the Spiritual Man continually, and then he is No Poet but a Heathen Philosopher at Enmity against all true Poetry or Inspiration.

An 1826 annotation to Wordsworth's *Poems*, vol. I, London, 1815, in *The Complete Writings of William Blake*, edited by Geoffrey Keynes, London: Oxford University Press, 1966, p. 782.

JOHN STUART MILL (1806-1873)

(i)

The difference, then, between the poetry of a poet, and the poetry of a cultivated but not naturally poetic mind, is, that in the latter, with how-ever bright a halo of feeling the thought may be surrounded and glorified, the thought itself is always the conspicuous object; while the poetry of a poet is Feeling itself, employing Thought only as a medium of its expression. In the one, feeling waits upon thought; in the other, thought upon feeling. The one writer has a distinct aim, common to him with any other didactic author; he desires to convey the thought, and he conveys it clothed in the feelings which it excites in himself, or which he deems most appropriate to it. The other merely pours forth the over-flowing of his feelings; and all the thoughts which those feelings suggest are floated promiscuously along the stream.

It may assist in rendering our meaning intelligible, if we illustrate it by a parallel between the two English authors of our own day, who have produced the greatest quantity of true and enduring poetry, Words-worth and Shelley. Apter instances could not be wished for; the one might be cited as the type, the *exemplar*, of what the poetry of culture may accomplish: the other as perhaps the most striking example ever known of the poetic temperament. How different, accordingly, is the poetry of these two great writers! In Wordsworth, the poetry is almost always the mere setting of a thought. The thought may be more valuable than the setting, or it may be less valuable, but there can be no question as to which was first in his mind: what he is impressed with, and what he is anxious to impress, is some proposition, more or less distinctly conceived; some truth, or something which he deems such. He lets the thought dwell in his mind, till it excites, as is the nature of thought, other thoughts, and also such feelings as the measure of his sensibility is adequate to supply. Among these thoughts and feelings, had he chosen a different walk of authorship (and there are many in which he might equally have excelled), he would probably have made a different selection of media for enforcing the parent thought: his habits, however, being those of poetic composition, he selects in preference the strongest feelings, and the thoughts with which most of feeling is naturally or habitually connected. His poetry, therefore, may be defined to be, his thoughts, coloured by, and impressing themselves by means of, emotions. Such poetry, Wordsworth has occupied a long life in producing. And well and wisely has he done so. Criticisms, no doubt, may be made occasionally both upon the thoughts themselves, and upon the skill he has demonstrated in the choice of his media: for, an affair of skill and study, in the most rigorous sense, it evidently was. But he has not laboured in vain: he has exercised, and continues to exercise, a powerful, and mostly a highly beneficial influence over the formation and growth of not a few of the most cultivated and vigorous of the youthful minds of our time, over whose heads poetry of the opposite description would have flown, for want of an original organization, physical or mental, in sympathy with it.

(ii)

What made Wordsworth's poems a medicine for my state of mind, was that they expressed, not mere outward beauty, but states of feeling, and of thought coloured by feeling, under the excitement of beauty. They seemed to be the very culture of the feelings, which I was in quest of. In them I seemed to draw from a source of inward joy, of sympathetic and imaginative pleasure, which could be shared in by all human beings; which had no connection with struggle or imperfection, but would be made richer by every improvement in the physical or social condition of mankind. From them I seemed to learn what would be the perennial sources of happiness, when all the greater evils of life shall have been removed. And I felt myself at once better and happier as I came under their influence. There have certainly been, even in our own age, greater poets than Wordsworth; but poetry of deeper and loftier feeling could not have done for me at that time what his did. I needed to be made to feel that there was real, permanent happiness in tranquil contemplation. Wordsworth taught me this not only without turning away from, but with a greatly increased interest in the common feelings and common destiny of human beings. And the delight which these poems gave me, proved that with culture of this sort, there was nothing to dread from the most confirmed habit of analysis. At the conclusion of the *Poems* came the famous Ode, falsely called Platonic, *Intimations of Immortality* in which, along with more than his usual sweetness of melody and rhythm, and along with the two passages of grand imagery but bad philosophy so often quoted, I found that he too had had similar experience to mine; that he also had felt that the first freshness of youthful enjoyment of life was not lasting; but that he had sought for compensation, and found it, in the way in which he was now teaching me to find it. The result was that I gradually, but completely, emerged from my habitual depression, and was never again subject to it. I long continued to value Wordsworth less according to his intrinsic merits, than by the measure of what he had done for me. Compared with the greatest poets, he may be said to be the poet of unpoetical natures, possessed of quiet and contemplative tastes. But unpoetical natures are precisely those which require poetic cultivation. This poetic cultivation Wordsworth is much more fitted to give, than poets who are intrinsically far more poets than he.

(i) From 'Thoughts on Poetry and Its Varieties' (1833), *Dissertations and Discussions*, 4 vols, London: Longmans, Green, Reader and Dyer, 1875, I, pp. 63–94 (83–4).
(ii) From *Autobiography* (1873), edited by Harold Laski, London: Oxford University Press, pp. 125–6. This passage describes an experience of 1828.

THOMAS DE QUINCEY (1785-1859)

But the great distinction of Wordsworth, and the pledge of his increasing popularity, is the extent of his sympathy with what is *really* permanent in human feelings, and also the depth of this sympathy. Young and Cowper, the two earlier leaders in the province of meditative poetry, are too circumscribed in the range of their sympathies, too narrow, too illiberal, and too exclusive. Both these poets manifested the quality of their strength in the quality of their public reception. Popular in some degree from the first, they entered upon the inheritance of their fame almost at once. Far different was the fate of Wordsworth: for in poetry of this class, which appeals to what lies deepest in man, in proportion to the native power of the poet, and his fitness for permanent life, is the strength of resistance in the public taste. Whatever is too original will be hated at the first. It must slowly mould a public for itself; and the resistance of the early thoughtless judgements must be overcome by a counter-resistance to itself in a better audience slowly mustering against the first. Forty and seven years it is since William Wordsworth first appeared as an author. Twenty of those years he was the scoff of the world, and his poetry a byword of scorn. Since then and more than once, senates have rung with acclamations to the echo of his name. Now, at this moment, whilst we are talking about him, he has entered upon his seventy-sixth year. For himself, according to the course of nature, he cannot be far from his setting; but his poetry is only now clearing the clouds that gathered about its rising. Meditative poetry is perhaps that province of literature which will ultimately maintain most power amongst the generations which are coming; but in this department, at least, there is little competition to be apprehended by Wordsworth from anything that has appeared since the death of Shakspere.

From 'On Wordsworth's Poetry' (1845), *The Collected Writings of Thomas De Quincey*, edited by David Masson, Edinburgh: Black, 1890, XI, pp. 321-2.

THOMAS BABINGTON MACAULAY (1800-1859)

I brought home and read *The Prelude*. It is a poorer *Excursion*, the same sort of faults and beauties; but the faults greater, and the beauties fainter, both in themselves and because faults are always made more offensive and beauties less pleasing by repetition. The story is the old story. There are the old raptures about mountains and cataracts; the old flimsy philosophy about the effect of scenery upon the mind; the old crazy, mystical metaphysics; the endless wilderness of dull, flat, prosaic twaddle; and here and there fine descriptions and energetic declamations interspersed.

From an entry in his *Journal* on July 1850. Quoted in Amy Cruse, *The Victorians and their Books*, London: Allen and Unwin, 1935, p. 177.

CHRISTOPHER WORDSWORTH (1807-1885)

The clue to his *poetical* theory [in *Lyrical Ballads*], in some of its more questionable details, may be found in his *political* principles; these had been democratical and still, though in some degree modified, they were of a republican character.

From *Memoirs of William Wordsworth*, 2 vols., London: Moxon, 1851, I,p. 125.

WALTER BAGEHOT (1826-1877)

He took a personal interest in the corners of the universe. There is a print of Rembrandt said to represent a piece of the Campagna, a mere waste, with a stump and a man, and under is written *'Tacet et loquitur'*, and thousands will pass the old print-shop where it hangs, and yet have a taste for paintings, and colours, and oils: but some fanciful students, some lonely stragglers, some long-haired enthusiasts, by chance will come, one by one, and look, and look, and be hardly able to take their eyes from the fascination, so massive is the shade, so still the conception, so firm the execution. Thus is it with Wordsworth and his poetry. *Tacet et loquitur*. Fashion apart, the million won't read it. Why should they?—they could not understand it,—don't put them out,—let them buy, and sell, and die,—but idle students, and enthusiastic wanderers, and solitary thinkers, will read, and read, and read, while their lives and their occupations hold. In truth, his works are the Scriptures of the intellectual life; for that same searching, and finding, and penetrating power which the real Scripture exercises on those engaged, as are the mass of men, in practical occupations and domestic ties, do his works exercise on the meditative, the solitary, and the young.

From 'Hartley Coleridge' (1852), *Literary Studies*, 3 vols., edited by R. H. Hutton, London: Longmans, Green, 1910, I, 1–36 (33).

MATTHEW ARNOLD (1822-1888)

. . . the fervent Wordsworthian will add, as Mr Leslie Stephen does, that Wordsworth's poetry is precious because his philosophy is sound; that his 'ethical system is as distinctive and capable of exposition as Bishop

Butler's, that his poetry is informed by ideas which fall spontaneously
into a scientific system of thought.' But we must be on our guard against
the Wordsworthians, if we want to secure for Wordsworth his due rank
as a poet. The Wordsworthians are apt to praise him for the wrong
things, and to lay far too much stress upon what they call his philosophy.
His poetry is the reality, his philosophy—so far, at least, as it may put
on the form and habit of 'a scientific system of thought', and the more
that it puts them on,—is the illusion. Perhaps we shall one day learn to
make this proposition general, and to say: Poetry is the reality, philosophy, the illusion. But in Wordsworth's case at any rate, we cannot do
him justice until we dismiss his formal philosophy.

The Excursion abounds with philosophy, and therefore *The Excursion*
is to the Wordsworthian what it can never be to the disinterested lover
of poetry,—a satisfactory work. 'Duty exists,' says Wordsworth, in
The Excursion; and then he proceeds thus:

> . . . Immutably survive,
> For our support, the measures and the forms,
> Which an abstract intelligence supplies,
> Whose kingdom is, where time and space are not.

And the Wordsworthian is delighted, and thinks here is a sweet union
of philosophy and poetry. But the disinterested lover of poetry will feel
that the lines carry us really not a step farther than the proposition
which they would interpret; that they are a tissue of elevated but
abstract verbiage, alien to the very nature of poetry.

Or let us come direct to the centre of Wordsworth's philosophy, as
'an ethical system, as distinctive and capable of systematical exposition
as Bishop Butler's':

> . . . One adequate support
> For the calamities of mortal life
> Exists, one only,—an assured belief
> That the procession of our fate, howe'er
> Sad or disturbed, is ordered by a Being
> Of infinite benevolence and power;
> Whose everlasting purposes embrace
> All accidents, converting them to good.

That is doctrine such as we hear in church too, religious and philosophic doctrine; and the attached Wordsworthian loves passages of
such doctrine, and brings them forward in proof of his poet's excellence.
But however true the doctrine may be, it has, as here presented, none
of the characters of *poetic* truth, the kind of truth which we require
from a poet, and in which Wordsworth is really strong.

Even the 'intimations' of the famous Ode, those cornerstones of the
supposed philosophic system of Wordsworth—the idea of the high

instincts and affections coming out in childhood, testifying of a divine home recently left, and fading away as our life proceeds,—this idea, of undeniable beauty as a play of fancy, has itself not the character of poetic truth of the best kind; it has no real solidity. The instinct of delight in Nature and her beauty has no doubt extraordinary strength in Wordsworth himself as a child. But to say that universally this instinct is mighty in childhood, and tends to die away afterwards, is to say what is extremely doubtful. In many people, perhaps with the majority of educated persons, the love of nature is nearly imperceptible at ten years old, but strong and operative at thirty. In general we may say of these high instincts of early childhood, the base of the alleged systematic philosophy of Wordsworth, what Thucydides says of the early achievements of the Greek race: 'It is impossible to speak with certainty of what is so remote; but from all that we can really investigate I should say that they were no very great things.'

Finally, the 'scientific system of thought' in Wordsworth gives us at last such poetry as this, which the devout Wordsworthian accepts:

> O for the coming of that glorious time
> When, prizing knowledge as her noblest wealth
> And best protection, this Imperial Realm,
> While she exacts allegiance, shall admit
> An obligation, on her part, to *teach*
> Them who are born to serve her and obey;
> Binding herself by statute to secure,
> For all the children whom her soil maintains,
> The rudiments of letters, and inform
> The mind with moral and religious truth.

Wordsworth calls Voltaire dull, and surely the production of these un-Voltairian lines must have been imposed on him as a judgment! One can hear them being quoted at a Social Science Congress; one can call up the whole scene. A great room in one of our dismal provincial towns; dusty air and jaded afternoon daylight; benches full of men with bald heads and women in spectacles; an orator lifting up his face from a manuscript written within and without to declaim these lines of Wordsworth; and in the soul of any poor child of nature who may have wandered in thither, an unutterable sense of lamentation, and mourning, and woe!

'But turn we', as Wordsworth says, 'from these bold, bad men' the haunters of Social Science Congresses. And let us be on our guard, too, against the exhibitors and extollers of a 'scientific system of thought' in Wordsworth's poetry. The poetry will never be seen aright while they thus exhibit it. The cause of its greatness is simple, and may be told quite simply. Wordsworth's poetry is great because of the extraordinary power with which Wordsworth feels the joy offered to us in nature, the joy offered to us in the simple primary affections and duties; and because of the extraordinary power with which, in case after case, he shows us this joy, and renders it so as to make us share it.

The source of joy from which he thus draws is the truest and most unfailing source of joy accessible to man. It is also accessible universally. Wordsworth brings us word, therefore, according to his own strong and characteristic line, he brings us word

Of joy in widest commonalty spread

Here is an immense advantage for a poet. Wordsworth tells of what all seek, and tells of it at its truest and best source, and yet a source where all may go and draw for it.

From 'Wordsworth' (1879 preface to *The Poems of Wordsworth*), *Essays in Criticism. First and Second Series* (Everyman edition), London: Dent, 1964, pp. 293–311 (304–7).

WILLIAM MINTO (writing in 1889)

It has often been remarked that although Wordsworth's long life extended to 1850, all his best work, with few exceptions, was done before 1808. He did not cease to write: he produced at least as much again in quantity: but there is a conspicuous falling off in quality. No external influence has been suggested to account for this; nothing has been spoken of but the premature diminution of his energy, or the hardening or stiffening of his faculties. We should probably not do wrong to connect it with the slow progress of the task on which his will was set as the great work of his life. To this task he addressed himself with resolute determination very soon after the publication of two thin volumes of minor pieces in 1807. These two volumes represent him in the very prime of his powers: they contain the 'Ode to Duty', the 'Intimations of Immortality', 'Resolution and Independence', 'Westminster Bridge', and the most powerful and inspiring of his political sonnets. This 1807 edition, indeed, is the *merum sal* of Wordsworth's genius; it is the most impressive single appeal that he ever made to the public, and remains still the best of all introductions to his poetry, better in its arrangement as it stands than any selection that has yet been made or could be made for the purpose. In it he would seem to have put his best before the public in the most attractive order that he could devise; and, that done, to have braced himself for the great work at which he had already made so many unprosperous and disheartening attempts. The result of several years of strenuous labour was *The Excursion*. The decline in his powers that has been so universally remarked coincides with his final entrance upon this unhappy task in full determination not to turn aside to right-hand or left till he had carried it through. It seems to me a most probable supposition that he

c

broke his spirit over it: that his vitality was sapped, the elasticity of his mind irretrievably impaired by a long continuance of comparatively joyless effort, by 'long-lived pressure of obscure distress'. He was far from being a self-complacent workman: the severe standard that he applied to the work of his contemporaries was applied with no less severity to his own work; no man knew better than himself that the sober moralizing of his interlocutors did not always, to use his own words, 'fulfil poetic conditions'. He said this of 'The Happy Warrior': how much more must he have felt it about many of the discourses of the Wanderer! And if he was disheartened on the completion of *The Prelude*, which is sustained throughout at a much higher poetic level, proceeds on a much simpler plan, and engaged him for less than half the time, we can hardly suppose that he looked back with satisfaction on *The Excursion*, a fragment, after all, of the projected *magnum opus*, a fragment after five years of continuous labour and seven more of vain beginnings and tentative bits. We must remember, too, that when *The Prelude* was completed, it was hailed with unbounded enthusiasm by Coleridge, and was not submitted to the cold criticism of an unsympathetic world. *The Excursion* was given to the world, and was received with protest and derision, while among the few friendly voices that came to encourage 'the lonely Muse', Coleridge's was not heard, but, on the contrary, was raised to express disappointment. Wordsworth would have been more than human if he had passed through such an ordeal with the buoyancy of his powers unimpaired. The magnificent sonnet to Haydon, 'High is our Calling, Friend', shows with how manly a spirit he bore his fate, but his undaunted faith in his mission, and the firm self-assertion with which he met the hostile critics who refused him what he felt to be his due, must not be confounded with serene indifference.

The result of any study of the history of *The Recluse* project must be to qualify considerably the conception of Wordsworth as a man of clear inflexible purpose, of steady, happy, self-satisfied industry, calmed and strengthened by the influence of Nature to pursue his aims with something of the self-absorption and indifference of Nature's own procedure. Persistency of purpose was undoubtedly his in an heroic degree, but to represent the relation between his conscious aims and his achievement as one of perfect harmony is to do violence to the facts. His conscious aims were vague and perplexed, and to a large extent perverse and unsuited to his powers. Nature laid her hand on him and guided him more wisely than he would have guided himself. His unconscious self was, under the guidance of Nature and circumstance, a greater poet than his conscious self aimed at being. There is no more striking instance in history of the narrowness of a great man's vision in laying plans for himself, or of the familiar truth that his ends are shaped for him, 'rough-hew them how he will'.

From 'Wordsworth's Great Failure', *The Nineteenth Century*, XXVI, 1889, pp. 434–51. Reprinted in *Wordsworth's Mind and Art*, edited by A. W. Thomson, Edinburgh: Oliver and Boyd, 1969, pp. 1–27 (25–7).

A. C. BRADLEY (1851-1935)

. . . the road into Wordsworth's mind must be through his strangeness and his paradoxes, and not round them. I do not mean that they are everywhere in his poetry. Much of it, not to speak of occasional platitudes, is beautiful without being peculiar or difficult; and some of this may be as valuable as that which is audacious or strange. But unless we get hold of that, we remain outside Wordsworth's centre; and, if we have not a most unusual affinity to him, we cannot get hold of that unless we realize its strangeness, and refuse to blunt the sharpness of its edge. Consider, for example, two or three of his statements; the statements of a poet, no doubt, and not of a philosopher, but still evidently statements expressing, intimating, or symbolizing, what for him was the most vital truth. He said that the meanest flower that blows could give him thoughts that often lie too deep for tears. He said, in a poem not less solemn, that Nature was the soul of all his moral being; and also that she can so influence us that nothing will be able to disturb our faith that all that we behold is full of blessings. After making his Wanderer tell the heart-rending tale of Margaret, he makes him say that the beauty and tranquillity of her ruined cottage had once so affected him

> That what we feel of sorrow and despair
> From ruin and from change, and all the grief
> The passing shows of Being leave behind,
> Appeared an idle dream, that could not live
> Where meditation was.

He said that this same Wanderer could read in the silent faces of the clouds unutterable love, and that among the mountains all things for him breathed immortality. He said to 'Almighty God',

> But thy most dreaded instrument
> For working out a pure intent
> Is Man arrayed for mutual slaughter;
> Yea, Carnage is thy daughter.

This last, it will be agreed, is a startling statement; but is it a whit more extraordinary than the others? It is so only if we assume that we are familiar with thoughts that lie too deep for tears, or if we translate 'the soul of all my moral being' into 'somehow concordant with my moral feelings', or convert 'all that we behold' into 'a good deal that we behold', or transform the Wanderer's reading of the silent faces of the

clouds into an argument from 'design'. But this is the road round
Wordsworth's mind, not into it.[1]

Again, with all Wordsworth's best poems, it is essential not to miss
the unique tone of his experience. This doubtless holds good of any true
poet, but not in the same way. With many poems there is little risk of
our failing either to feel what is distinctive of the writer, or to appropriate what he says. What is characteristic, for example, in Byron's
lines, *On this day I complete my thirty-sixth year*, or in Shelley's *Stanzas
written in dejection near Naples*, cannot escape discovery, nor is there any
difficulty in understanding the mood expressed. But with Wordsworth,
for most readers, this risk is constantly present in some degree. Take,
for instance, one of the most popular of his lyrics, the poem about the
daffodils by the lake. It is popular partly because it remains a pretty
thing even to those who convert it into something quite undistinctive
of Wordsworth. And it is comparatively easy, too, to perceive and to
reproduce in imagination a good deal that *is* distinctive; for instance,
the feeling of the sympathy of the waves and the flowers and the breeze
in their glee, and the Wordsworthian 'emotion recollected in tranquillity' expressed in the lines (written by his wife),

> They flash upon that inward eye
> Which is the bliss of solitude.

But there remains something still more intimately Wordsworthian:

> I wandered lonely as a Cloud
> That floats on high o'er vales and hills.

It is thrust into the reader's face, for these are the opening lines. But
with many readers it passes unheeded, because it is strange and outside
their own experience. And yet it is absolutely essential to the effect of
the poem.

This poem, however, even when thoroughly conventionalized, would
remain, as I said, a pretty thing; and it could scarcely excite derision.
Our point is best illustrated from the pieces by which Wordsworth most
earned ridicule, the ballad poems. They arose almost always from some
incident which, for him, had a novel and arresting character and came
on his mind with a certain shock; and if we do not get back to this
through the poem, we remain outside it. We may, of course, get back
to this and yet consider the poem to be more or less a failure. There is

---

[1] These statements, with the exception of the last, were chosen partly because
they all say, with the most manifest seriousness, much the same thing that is
said, with a touch of playful exaggeration, in *The Tables Turned*, where occurs
that outrageous stanza about 'one impulse from a vernal wood' which Mr
Raleigh has well defended. When all fitting allowance has been made for the fact
that these statements, and many like them, are 'poetic,' they ought to remain
startling. Two of them—that from the story of Margaret (*Excursion*, I.), and that
from the *Ode*, 1815—were made less so, to the injury of the passages, by the
Wordsworth of later days, who had forgotten what he felt, or yielded to the
objections of others.

here therefore room for legitimate differences of opinion. Mr Swinburne sees, no doubt, as clearly as Coleridge did, the intention of *The Idiot Boy* and *The Thorn*, yet he calls them 'doleful examples of eccentricity in dullness', while Coleridge's judgement, though he criticized both poems, was very different. I believe (if I may venture into the company of such critics) that I see why Wordsworth wrote *Goody Blake and Harry Gill* and the *Anecdote for Fathers*, and yet I doubt if he has succeeded in either; but a great man, Charles James Fox, selected the former for special praise, and Matthew Arnold included the latter in a selection from which he excluded *The Sailor's Mother*.[2] Indeed, of all the poems at first most ridiculed there is probably not one that has not been praised by some excellent judge. But they were ridiculed by men who judged them without attempting first to get inside them. And this is fatal.

From 'Wordsworth', *Oxford Lectures on Poetry*, London: Macmillan, 1959 (first published 1909), pp. 99–148 (101–5).

H. W. GARROD (1878–1960)

'There is a change, and I am poor'. The words are truer than Wordsworth meant them to be, or at any rate, far wider in their application. He is speaking of the affections. But he is poorer, not only in the wealth of the affections, but in the riches of philosophic thought; and there lie before him more than forty years of this philosophic and poetic poverty—a long period illuminated now and again by flashes of the old vision, but in the main lamentably dull and drab, the most dismal anticlimax of which the history of literature holds record.

No one who has followed with any attention what has already been said of the metaphysical theories which lie behind Wordsworth's poetry will have failed to perceive in connexion with these a great deal that is left inchoate and, indeed, confused. In particular, in respect of the relation of the imagination to the logical reason many, or rather most, of the questions that present themselves remain undetermined. The two powers confront one another in a sort of armed neutrality.

---

[2] *Goody Blake*, to my mind, tries vainly to make the kind of impression overwhelmingly made by Coleridge's *Three Graves*. The question as to the *Anecdote for Fathers* is not precisely whether it makes you laugh, but whether it makes you laugh at the poet, and in such a way that the end fails to restore your sobriety. The danger is in the lines,

And five times to the child I said,
Why, Edward, tell my why?

The reiteration, with the struggle between the poet and his victim, is thoroughly Wordsworthian, and there are cases where it is managed with perfect success, as we shall see; but to me it has here the effect so delightfully reproduced in *Through the Looking-glass* ('I'll tell thee everything I can').

With the forces of the imagination are leagued those of the senses; but as between the forms given to the senses and those rendered back by the imagination, it is not always easy to divine which are the shadows and which the substance. I have the feeling that amid the philosophic doubts which Wordsworth had thus raised for himself, and us, he stood, in 1807, in a situation more perplexed than either his pride could allow or his unaided reflections expedite. Perhaps only Coleridge could have helped him—Coleridge with his careless gift (to no one more acceptable than to Wordsworth) of bestowing benefits with the fine air of a man who receives them. Coleridge was, in any case, one of those minds which startle other minds out of the *ordinariness* which so easily besets most men, and besets at fitful intervals even genius. We have noticed already how Wordsworth was conscious of, and even emphasizes the presence of, a certain ordinariness in his own nature and habits. He saw himself as in general a very boyish boy, and again as a very average under-graduate, and yet again as a youth like so many others, vacillating between rebellion and listlessness. Yet he beheld always, as it were, a silver thread of 'vision' variegating this ordinariness, in all periods of its manifestation. Coleridge also saw the ordinariness. He lamented in Wordsworth, says Hazlitt, 'a something corporeal, a matter-of-factness, a clinging to the palpable'. Nor did it, as we all know, escape the observation of De Quincey, who so often, in his account of Words-worth, replaces the poet by the shrewd and hard-headed and somewhat contentious Dalesman. Coleridge, as I say, was one of those men in whose presence it is difficult to be ordinary. He had (with whatever faults) that generosity of temper which rouses others to their proper greatness—the mere sound of his voice was, as Hazlitt says, 'the music of thought'. The withdrawal of his influence carried with it, for Words-worth, not only, as I think, philosophical impoverishment, but a kind of relapse into ordinariness. From 1807 on, Wordsworth sinks deeper and deeper into ordinariness—like a man relapsing into some sensual indulgence; he drugs himself with the humdrum of political and social and religious orthodoxy; and only now and again, in some mysteriously appointed casual re-awakening, does he shake off the influence—else ever intensifying—of the deadly opiate.

If these seem depressing reflections, yet they have this much in them that is re-fortifying: that of a world, where so much proceeds by rule of thumb, one of the facts, none the less, is the being of genius; of which the principal character is its dominant unpredictability. Those who believe in it, who believe that there really and truly is an order of inspired men, having qualities actually different in kind from those of other men, have small reason to be either surprised or affronted as they mark in poets the odd comings and goings of their greatness and dull-ness. It is no little thing, after all, if over a period of ten years we can detain an unintermitted fullness of inspired being.

From *Wordsworth: Lectures and Essays* (based on lectures of 1919), Oxford: Clarendon Press, 1927 (second edition), pp. 138–40.

SALVADOR DE MADARIAGA (writing in 1920)

Wordsworth is the poorest in rhythm of all great English poets. Indeed, that is not saying enough, for English poetry is exceptionally rich in rhythm. It is doubtful whether Wordsworth had even a clear idea of what rhythm is. Whenever he theorizes on poetry, he refers only to rhyme and metre. Now, metre is to rhythm what the seven notes of the piano are to music, or the five lines of the score to the notes printed on them. Wordsworth does not seem to have understood the difference between the 'score' of metrical arrangements, conventional though based on natural laws, and the spontaneous song of rhythm playing on it. This is a hard saying and one which cannot be advanced without diffidence. Yet, it is not easy to interpret otherwise the lack of rhythm, or worse still, of correspondence between rhythm and matter, in his writings, and the direct evidence on the subject which he left in his prose works. It will be remembered that in his famous criticism of Gray's sonnet,[1] referring to the lines:

I fruitless mourn to him that cannot hear
And weep the more because I weep in vain,

he says:

'It will easily be perceived that the only part of this sonnet which is is of any value is the lines printed in italics; it is equally obvious that, except in the rhyme, and in the use of the single word "fruitless" for fruitlessly, which is so far a defect, the language of these lines does in no respect differ from that of prose.'

This example goes far to show that Wordsworth was deaf to rhythm and saw nothing in poetry but metre and rhyme, and that 'harmony in numbers' which derives from the mere flow of language between the banks of metre. But, if there were any doubt as to what he meant by this word *metre*, so often under his pen, metre, as he says, 'regulated by strict laws', he has left numerous passages, any one of which should suffice to prove that he did not realize the existence in poetry of a spontaneous and substantial element of music above the adventitious and instrumental element of metrical arrangements. Thus, he has an ingenious theory of the soothing effect of the 'continual and regular impulses of pleasurable surprise from the metrical arrangement' which he gives as proof of the utility of metre to make more bearable 'the most pathetic scenes' of Shakespeare. He thinks of metre as of a merely adventitious element which the writer can if he so desires 'superadd' (the very word is a final argument). He says as much in as clear a language as we can desire. 'Metre is but adventitious to composition.' Or, 'Now, supposing for a moment that whatever is interesting in these

[1] 'Observations to the Second Edition of the Lyrical Ballads.'

objects may be as vividly described in prose, why am I to be condemned
if to such description I have endeavoured to superadd the charm which
by the consent of all nations is acknowledged to exist in metrical
language?' And again: 'To this language [that of the earliest poets] it is
probable that metre of some sort or other was early superadded.'

He thought apparently that the word *singing* applied to poets was a
metaphor and does not seem to have suspected its accurate and literal
meaning . . . he was representative of the British race, and particularly of
the British gentleman. It is indeed a quality in a man; it is a defect in a
truthseeker.

Most of Wordsworth's poems, particularly those in which the purpose
is more manifest, suffer from this unconscious limitation of his outlook.
A typical example is the poem generally known today as 'The Leech-
Gatherer', but perhaps more accurately described under its old title,
'Resolution and Independence'. Here is a comfortable country gentleman, 'a traveller upon the moor', who, for sheer excess of joy, is
suddenly seized by a fit of depression. He comes upon a poor old man.

> The oldest man he seemed that ever wore grey hairs,

so old and life-beaten that

> His body was bent double, feet and head
> Coming together in life's pilgrimage.

The gentleman inquires:

> What occupation do you there pursue?

He is a leech-gatherer. That is his occupation.

> Employment hazardous and wearisome.

A striking contrast. All fortune's smiles on one side. All fate's burdens
on the other. Our poet might have been impressed with the view of life
which the old man would have contemplated had he known all the
facts; or he might have risen above the two sides and reflected on the
futility of it all, and exclaimed with La Bruyère: 'On a honte d'être
heureux en face de certaines misères.' But no. Our poet has *his* own
world to put in order, his own house to build, his own axe to grind. He
has not a single thought for the old man as he really is, and therefore not
one single feeling for him. He immediately starts thinking about himself with such self-centred distraction that, as he says:

> The old man still stood talking by my side;
> But now his voice to me was like a stream
> Scarce heard; nor word from word could I divide,

and, *giving* him nothing, not even the courtesy of listening, he *takes*
from him comfort for his fit of depression—his depression which was a
mere surfeit of joy:

and when he ended,
I could have laughed myself to scorn to find
In that decrepit man so firm a mind.
'God!' said I, 'be my help and stay secure.
I'll think of the leech-gatherer on the lonely moor!'

It is impossible to carry the self-protective instinct further. Who could successfully attack such a citadel of pleasant thought? For there was only one possible way of extracting an optimistic impression from the incident, and that was to concentrate on the 'resolution and independence' of the old man, and to suppress all the painful thoughts and feelings which would have grieved a more fraternal and less guarded heart at the sight of such pathetic adversity.

It should be noticed, moreover, that in this poem Wordsworth deliberately distorts reality in order to adjust it to his preconceived plan. We know through Dorothy Wordsworth's Journal that the meeting with the old man took place on the road to Grasmere, not 'on the lonely moor'. As Professor Raleigh says, 'Wordsworth shifts the scene in order to show the old man at his work, and to set him among elemental powers akin to his majestic and indomitable spirit.' In doing so, the poet was within his rights. He was in fact showing great dramatic skill. But the eminent critic adds: 'For the rest, the record is true enough', and here it is, I am afraid, impossible to agree with him. Far from being 'true enough', the poem differs from the facts in one essential respect, namely, that the 'resolution and independence' of which Wordsworth made the substance of his poem only existed in his imagination. The leech-gatherer of the poem says that leeches have become scarce,

Yet still I persevere and find them where I may.

But let us turn to Dorothy Wordsworth who had no poem to write and no lesson to teach:

'His trade was to gather leeches, but now leeches were scarce, and he had not strength for it. He lived by begging, and was making his way to Carlisle, where he should buy a few godly books to sell.'[2]

Begging is not independence, and 'not having strength for it' is not resolution. It will be seen therefore that Wordsworth 'made up' not merely the scenery but the very substance of his poem. No one would find fault with this, were he engaged in a purely æsthetic task. But that is not the case. 'Resolution and Independence' was written *in order to* justify optimism by means of feelings supposed to be taken from nature. Fidelity to nature is, and must be, on his own theory, the first condition of Wordsworth's work. In this case the image supplied by nature was so *refracted* by Wordsworth's brain as to appear upside down. The result is a false poem, a poem which, though professing to be born out of an

---

[2] Dorothy Wordsworth's Journal, 3 October 1800.

emotion actually felt, is wholly invented—a typical example of that
cerebral poetry in which Wordsworth habitually indulged, written in
such a mood that the heart does not inspire the brain, but the brain
forces and drives the heart to feeling. And that is why the 'Leech-
Gatherer', despite some passages of lofty eloquence, cannot be counted
as a work of art. It is an anecdote, deliberate, prejudiced and
overstrained.

From 'The Case of Wordsworth', *Shelley and Calderon and Other
Essays on English and Spanish Poetry*, London: Constable, 1920,
pp. 126–90 (138–40, 162–5).

ALDOUS HUXLEY (1894-1963)

It is only very occasionally that he admits the existence in the world
around him of those 'unknown modes of being' of which our immediate
intuitions of things make us so disquietingly aware. Normally what he
does is to pump the dangerous Unknown out of Nature and refill the
emptied forms of hills and woods, flowers and waters, with something
more reassuringly familiar—with humanity, with Anglicanism. He will
not admit that a yellow primrose is simply a yellow primrose—beautiful,
but essentially strange, having its own alien life apart. He wants
it to possess some sort of soul, to exist humanly, not simply
flowerily. He wants the earth to be more than earthy, to be a
divine person. But the life of vegetation is radically unlike the life of
man: the earth has a mode of being that is certainly not the mode of
being of a person. 'Let Nature be your teacher,' says Wordsworth. The
advice is excellent. But how strangely he himself puts it into practice!
Instead of listening humbly to what the teacher says, he shuts his ears
and himself dictates the lesson he desires to hear. The pupil knows
better than his master; the worshipper substitutes his own oracles for
those of the god. Instead of accepting the lesson as it is given to his
immediate intuitions, he distorts it rationalistically into the likeness of a
parson's sermon or a professorial lecture. Our direct intuitions of Nature
tell us that the world is bottomlessly strange: alien, even when it is kind
and beautiful; having innumerable modes of being that are not our
modes; always mysteriously not personal, not conscious, not moral;
often hostile and sinister; sometimes even unimaginably, because
inhumanly, evil. In his youth, it would seem, Wordsworth left his direct
intuitions of the world unwarped.

> The sounding cataract
> Haunted me like a passion: the tall rock,
> The mountain, and the deep and gloomy wood,
> Their colours and their forms, were then to me
> An appetite; a feeling and a love,

That had no need of a remoter charm,
By thought supplied, nor any interest Unborrowed from the eye.

As the years passed, however, he began to interpret them in terms of a preconceived philosophy. Procrustes-like, he tortured his feelings and perceptions until they fitted his system. . . .

The change in Wordsworth's attitude towards Nature is symptomatic of his general apostasy. Beginning as what I may call a natural aesthete, he transformed himself, in the course of years, into a moralist, a thinker. He used his intellect to distort his exquisitely acute and subtle intuitions of the world, to explain away their often disquieting strangeness, to simplify them into a comfortable metaphysical unreality. Nature had endowed him with the poet's gift of seeing more than ordinarily far into the brick walls of external reality, of intuitively comprehending the character of the bricks, of feeling the quality of their being, and establishing the appropriate relationship with them. But he preferred to think his gifts away. He preferred, in the interests of a preconceived religious theory, to ignore the disquieting strangeness of things, to interpret the impersonal diversity of Nature in terms of a divine, anglican unity. He chose, in a word, to be a philosopher, comfortably at home with a man-made and, therefore, thoroughly comprehensible system, rather than a poet adventuring for adventure's sake through the mysterious world revealed by his direct and undistorted intuitions.

From 'Wordsworth in the Tropics', *Do What You Will*, London: Chatto and Windus, 1929, pp. 113–29 (pp. 117–18, 127–8).

Modern Critics on Wordsworth

T. S. ELIOT

What all the fuss was about

. . . And much of the poetry of Wordsworth and Coleridge is just as turgid and artificial and elegant as any eighteenth century die-hard could wish. What then was all the fuss about?

There really was something to make a fuss about. I do not know whether Professor Garrod has grasped it, but if so he seems to ignore it; Professor Harper,[1] however, seems to have it by the right lug. There is a remarkable letter of Wordsworth's in 1801 which he wrote to Charles James Fox in sending him a copy of the *Ballads*. You will find a long extract from this letter in Professor Harper's book. I quote one sentence. In commending his poems to the fashionable politician's attention Wordsworth says:

> 'Recently by the spreading of manufactures through every part of the country, by the heavy taxes upon postage, by workhouses, houses of industry, and the invention of soup shops, etc., superadded to the increasing disproportion between the price of labour and that of the necessaries of life, the bonds of domestic feeling among the poor, as far as the influence of these things has extended, have been weakened, and in innumerable instances entirely destroyed.'

Wordsworth then proceeds to expound a doctrine which nowadays is called distributism. And Wordsworth was not merely taking advantage of an opportunity to lecture a rather disreputable statesman and rouse him to useful activity; he was seriously explaining the content and purpose of his poems: without this preamble Mr Fox could hardly be expected to make head or tail of the Idiot Boy or the sailor's parrot. You may say that this public spirit is irrelevant to Wordsworth's greatest poems; nevertheless I believe that you will understand a great poem like 'Resolution and Independence' better if you understand the purposes and social passions which animated its author; and unless you understand these you will misread Wordsworth's literary criticism

[1] In his Life of Wordsworth.

entirely. Incidentally, those who speak of Wordsworth as the original Lost Leader (a reference which Browning, as I remember, denied) should make pause and consider that when a man takes politics and social affairs seriously the difference between revolution and reaction may be by the breadth of a hair, and that Wordsworth may possibly have been no renegade but a man who thought, so far as he thought at all, for himself. But it is Wordsworth's social interest that inspires his own novelty of form in verse, and backs up his explicit remarks upon poetic diction; and it is really this social interest which (consciously or not) the fuss was all about. It was not so much from lack of thought as from warmth of feeling that Wordsworth originally wrote the words 'the language of conversation in middle and lower class society'. It was not from any recantation of political principles, but from having had it brought to his attention that, as a general literary principle, this would never do, that he altered them. Where he wrote 'my purpose was to imitate, and as far as possible, to adopt, the very language of men' he was saying what no serious critic could disapprove.

Except on this point of diction, and that of 'choosing incidents from common life', Wordsworth is a most orthodox critic. It is true that he uses the word 'enthusiasm' which the eighteenth century did not like, but in the matter of mimesis he is more deeply Aristotelian than some who have aimed at following Aristotle more closely. He says of the poet:

'To these qualities he has added a disposition to be affected more than other men by absent things as if they were present; an ability of conjuring up in himself passions, which are indeed far from being the same as those produced by real events, yet (especially in those parts of the general sympathy which are pleasing and delightful) do more nearly resemble the passions produced by real events, than anything which, from the motions of their own minds merely, other men are accustomed to feel in themselves.'

Here is the new version of Imitation, and I think that it is the best so far:

'Aristotle, I have been told, has said, that Poetry is the most philosophic of all writing; it is so: its object is truth, not individual and local, but general, and operative.'

I find that 'it is so' very exhilarating. For my part, rather than be parrotted by a hundred generations, I had rather be neglected and have one man eventually come to my conclusions and say 'there is an old author who found this out before I did'.

When you find Wordsworth as the seer and prophet whose function it is to instruct and edify through pleasure, as if this were something he had found out for himself, you may begin to think that there is something in it, at least for some kinds of poetry. Some portions of this enthusiasm I believe Wordsworth communicated to Coleridge. But Wordsworth's revolutionary faith was more vital to him than it was to

Coleridge. You cannot say that it inspired his revolution in poetry, but it cannot be disentangled from the motives of his poetry. Any radical change in poetic form is likely to be the symptom of some very much deeper change in society and in the individual. I doubt whether the impulse in Coleridge would have been strong enough to have worked its way out, but for the example and encouragement of Wordsworth. I would not be understood as affirming that revolutionary enthusiasm is the best parent for poetry, or as justifying revolution on the ground that it will lead to an outburst of poetry—which would be a wasteful, and hardly justifiable way of producing poetry. Nor am I indulging in sociological criticism, which has to suppress so much of the data, and which is ignorant of so much of the rest. I only affirm that all human affairs are involved with each other, that consequently all history involves abstraction, and that in attempting to win a full understanding of the poetry of a period you are led to the consideration of subjects which at first sight appear to have little bearing upon poetry.

From 'Wordsworth and Coleridge', *The Use of Poetry and the Use of Criticism*, London: Faber and Faber, 1933, pp. 67–85 (72–6).

Wordsworth and the Locke Tradition

Wordsworth was the kind of poet who could only have appeared at the end of the eighteenth century, when mythologies were exploded, and a belief in the visible universe as the body of which God was the soul alone remained. In this sense his beliefs can be viewed as data furnished to him by a tradition; in this sense he, as well as Dante, may be said to have employed his sensibility within a framework of received beliefs. But his debt to tradition, unlike Dante's, was a negative one; he owed to it his *deprivation* of mythology, his aloneness with the universe. His more positive beliefs, those by which he appears in reaction against the scientific tradition, were built up by him out of his own poetic experiences, and it is this which makes him representative of the modern situation—the situation in which beliefs are made out of poetry rather than poetry out of beliefs. To animize the 'real' world, the 'universe of death' that the 'mechanical' system of philosophy had produced, but to do so without either using an exploded mythology or fabricating a new one, this was the special task and mission of Wordsworth. Wordsworth's conviction that the human mind was capable of this task was the most important of his 'positive' beliefs, and this belief he owed chiefly to his own experiences. It is this which distinguishes his 'deism' from that of, for instance, Thomson's *Seasons*, to which it bears an obvious superficial resemblance. For Thomson, as for Pope, mythologies were almost as 'unreal' as for Wordsworth, but their positive belief, their Deism (in so far as they genuinely held it), was 'intellectually' held, and it consequently appears in poetry mainly as rhetoric. The poetry exists to decorate, to render agreeable, a set of abstract notions; and these abstractions have been taken over, as truth, from the natural philosophers—from Descartes, Newton, Locke, or Leibnitz. Wordsworth's beliefs, on the other hand, were largely the formulation of his own dealings with 'substantial things'; they were held intellectually only because they had first been 'proved upon the pulses'. That the result of his 'dealings' was not a *Divine Comedy* or a *Paradise Lost* was due, we may say, to the scientific movement and the sensationalist philosophy of Locke and Hartley; that the result was not an *Essay on Man*, a *Seasons*, or a *Botanic Garden* was due to himself. For it was the 'visible world', no abstract machine, that Wordsworth sought; and he felt that mechanical materialism had substituted a 'universe of death for that

which moves with light and life instinct, actual, divine, and true'.[1]
The belief that Wordsworth constructed out of his experiences was a
belief in the capacity of the mind to co-operate with this 'active
universe', to contribute something of its own to it in perceiving it, and
not, as sensationalism taught, merely to receive, passively, impressions
from without. It was this belief, or the experiences upon which the
belief was based, which encouraged him to hope that poetry might be
delivered from the fetters of the mechanical tradition without being
allowed to fall into disrepute as 'unreal' or 'fanciful.' . . . Wordsworth's
poetic activity, then, was largely conditioned by the 'reality-standards'
of his time, which left him alone with the visible universe. But his
'creative sensibility' had taught him that he was not alone with an
'inanimate cold world', but with an 'active universe', a universe capable
of being moulded and modified by the 'plastic power' which abode
within himself. As long as he could be a poet, this belief in the bond
between man and nature was valid. Poetry becomes, with Wordsworth,
the record of moments of 'ennobling interchange of action from within
and from without';[2] it takes on, in fine, a *psychological* aspect. 'There is
scarcely one of my poems', Wordsworth wrote to Lady Beaumont,
'which does not aim to direct the attention to some moral sentiment, or
to some general principle, or law of thought, or of our intellectual
constitution.'[3]

I have emphasised this 'aloneness' of Wordsworth with the universe,
because I think it marks his position in the history of 'poetry and
beliefs', and because it seems to determine the quality of much of his
work. Centuries of intellectual development had now brought matters
to this, that if poetry were still to be made, it must be made by the sheer
unaided power of the individual poet. And what was it that he must
make? A record of successes; of successful imaginative dealings with the
world of eye and ear. And what was to be the criterion of success? That
plastic power shall have been exerted upon the 'vulgar forms of every
day', but in such a way that there shall be no departure from 'nature's
living images'. The midnight storm may grow darker in presence of the
poet's eye, the visionary dreariness, the consecration, may be spread
over sea or land, but the transforming power must work 'subservient
strictly to external things'; there must be intensification without dis-
tortion. Fact and value were to be combined in this 'fine balance of
truth in observing, with the imaginative faculty in modifying, the object
observed'. But what sort of 'truth' may be claimed for the creation
which world and mind 'with blended might accomplish'?—for, that
poetry is 'the most philosophic of all writing', that 'its object is truth', is
Wordsworth's profound conviction.[4] I suppose the answer would be,
'psychological' truth; that is to say, the poetry is faithfully expressive of

[1] *The Prelude*, XIV. 160.
[2] *The Prelude*, XIII. 375.
[3] In *Wordsworth's Literary Criticism* (Oxford, 1905), p.51.
[4] *Lyrical Ballads*, Pref., p. 25 in *Wordsworth's Literary Criticism*.

D

certain states of consciousness. Of the two elements of which these states are composed, fact and value, Wordsworth is equally sure of both. He is sure of the fact, because he knows no man has observed it more intently; he is sure of the value, because this was intuitively apprehended in himself, it came from within. He is no less sure of the truth of the resulting creation, because it had been experienced as a modification of his own consciousness. But it was only as long as his mind was dealing thus nakedly with observed fact that Wordsworth could feel this conviction of truthfulness. Any translation of his experience into myth, personification or fable, though not necessarily always culpable, is inevitably a lapse towards a lower level of truth, a fall, in fact, from imagination to fancy. Poetry exists to transform, to make this much-loved earth more lovely; and in former times men could express their sense of fact, without misgiving, in mythologies. But since the coming of the enlightened age this was becoming almost impossible. The efforts of eighteenth century poets to vitalize the dead matter of the Cartesian universe by using the symbols of an outworn mythology had ended in fiasco, and the abandonment of the symbols, at any rate for a time, became a necessity.

But this abandonment threw upon Wordsworth, as it throws still more emphatically upon the contemporary poet, an enormous burden, no less, in fact, than 'the weight of all this unintelligible world'. He must be continually giving proofs of strength in order to maintain his belief that the load *could* be lightened. To keep the vast encompassing world from becoming 'cold and inanimate' by transferring to it a 'human and intellectual life' from the poet's own spirit; to 'dissolve, diffuse, and dissipate in order to re-create'; to 'idealize, and to unify', to 'shoot one's being through earth, air and sea'—what a stupendous task for the un-aided spirit of man! Is it to be wondered at that Wordsworth, after bearing the heavy and the weary weight, Atlas-like, for many years, should at last, like Atlas, have turned into a mountain of stone? Youth, and Coleridge, and Dorothy, and the moonlight of Alfoxden—these could and did lighten the burden for him for a while. But there are many signs that after this his material began to resist him more and more stubbornly. Was there not something in the very nature of the poetic task he had set himself which made this inevitable? 'To spread the tone, the atmosphere, and with it the depth and height of the ideal world around forms, incidents and situations, of which, for the common view, custom had bedimmed all the lustre, had dried up the sparkle and the dew-drops'[5]—this is probably the special prerogative of youth. In youth the imagination poured the modifying colours prodigally over all things, and only when its vitality began to sink did the man discover how much virtue had been going out of him. With the realisation that 'objects *as* objects, are essentially fixed and dead', comes the disturbing sense that 'in our life alone does nature live'. That Wordsworth had

[5] Coleridge, *Biog. Lit.*, ch. V. vol. I. p. 59. The other quoted phrases on this and the former page are also Coleridge's.

reached this point at about the age of thirty-five is fairly clear from the passage in Book XII. of *The Prelude*, where, echoing Coleridge, he declares

'That from thyself it comes, that thou must give,
Else never canst receive.'[6]

The whole context from which these words are taken shows also how habitually, by this time, Wordsworth had come to find in *memory* his chief reservoir of strength. Certain memories are the 'hiding-places of man's power'; memories, that is, of former successful exertions of imaginative strength. In *The Prelude* pre-eminently, though elsewhere as well, Wordsworth, now fighting a losing battle with *das Gemeine*, supported his strength for a while by drawing upon the past. But he was living upon capital, and when that was spent, what was to remain?

From 'Postscript: On Wordsworth and the Locke Tradition', *The Seventeenth Century Background*, London: Chatto and Windus, 1942, pp. 296–309 (298–300, 304–7).

[6] *The Prelude*, XII. 276.

PATRICK CRUTTWELL

Wordsworth, the Public and the People

In 1807 Wordsworth published a two-volume collection of his poems, his first since the later editions of *Lyrical Ballads*. Much of his best work is in it—'Resolution and Independence', for example, the sonnets on Westminster Bridge, and 'The world is too much with us . . .', and the 'Immortality' ode—and much of his characteristic inseparable worst, such as the Spade! with which Wilkinson had till'd his lands. Whether because of the former or the latter, the volumes met with a critical reception at best disappointed, at worst derisive. The verdict of Samuel Rogers—great talents shamefully misapplied—seems to have been the general decision; Miss Anna Seward, the Swan of Lichfield, a lady of extreme sensibility and high cultivation who may stand as representative of the bluestocking tribe, decided in a letter to Walter Scott that 'surely Wordsworth must be mad as was ever the poet Lee . . . this egotistic manufacturer' (she continues) 'of metaphysic importance upon trivial themes'[1]; and Scott himself, though he liked and admired Wordsworth's character and some of his verse, was compelled to agree. 'But many of Wordsworth's lesser poems are *caviare*, not only to the multitude, but to all who judge of poetry by the established rules of criticism.'[2] These were the private verdicts of literary individuals; what Wordsworth read in public print was no more agreeable, for the *Critical Review* produced what its victim called 'a miserable heap of spiteful nonsense',[3] and Jeffrey in the *Edinburgh* for October 1807, feeling as he did 'indignation and compassion, at that strange infatuation which has bound him up from the fair exercise of his talents', concluded by 'venturing to hope, that there is now an end to this folly'. It is true that all these verdicts were more or less qualified by approvals of particular poems, but every author knows that what one broods on in the small hours is the verdict itself, not the pleas for mitigation of sentence.

Wordsworth was hurt, as any author would be, by this chorus of disapproval. His own claim to be 'as insensible as iron to these petty stings'[4] was true on the highest level—for nothing on earth would turn Wordsworth from what he believed to be his right direction—but on

1 Letter of 24 August 1807.
2 Letter to Southey of November 1807.
3 Letter to Francis Wrangham of 4 November 1807.
4 Letter to Lady Beaumont of 21 May 1807.

all other levels he was thoroughly shaken. And also, it is likely, taken aback; for *Lyrical Ballads* had been, as Dorothy remarks and even Jeffrey admitted,[5] surprisingly popular. It looks as if the *Poems* of 1807 forced into public notice some things about Wordsworth which *Lyrical Ballads* had only hinted at, as if the implications of Wordsworth's Preface had sunk at last into the general consciousness. Here, it seemed, was a crew of silly poets, with Wordsworth the silliest at their head, writing silly little poems, which broke all 'the established laws of poetry' (the phrase is Jeffrey's), about the domestic misfortunes of uninteresting rustics. The new publication acted as a trigger; volleys of protest, long prepared-for, were now fired off. And they did penetrate. They increased for one thing, Wordsworth's long-standing reluctance to publish; for in 1808 Dorothy had to urge him on to publish *The White Doe of Ryl-stone*—'As for the outcry against you, I would defy it. . . . Do, dearest William! do pluck up your Courage and overcome your disgust to publishing'[6]—but in fact the *White Doe* was not published until seven years later. Wordsworth was hurt and shocked; he was also bewildered. His bewilderment drove him, in the months after these volumes' publication, to think more deeply and anxiously than ever before about the relations between himself and his readers. Something had clearly gone wrong; there was a failure to understand, a failure to communicate. But Wordsworth was desperately anxious to communicate; he was neither a mystic, for whom his own vision would be enough, nor an entertainer, who could change his act if the audience threw things. He was a preacher, who must have an audience but must have it on his own terms only. 'Every great poet is a Teacher: I wish either to be considered as a Teacher or as nothing.'[7] 'An affair of whole continents of moral sympathy'[8] was what he asked for: a large demand, but inevitable, by the very nature of his poetry.

A teacher without pupils, a demander of moral sympathy who finds no sympathizers? They would never be found—it had now become clear to him—not among the ordinary readers and writers, never in the literary world. That world he christens 'the Public', surrounding his use of the word with scornful qualifications: 'what is called the Public', 'that portion of my contemporaries who are called the Public'.[9] They are urban, they are fashionable; 'all worldlings of every rank and situation' are among them. They suffer from a 'pure absolute honest ignorance' of 'the thoughts, feelings, and images, on which the life of

[5] Dorothy in a letter to Jane Marshall of 10 September 1800: 'The first volume sold much better than we expected, and was liked by a much greater number of people.' Jeffrey in his review of the *Poems* of 1807: 'The Lyrical Ballads were unquestionably popular, and, we have no hesitation in saying, deservedly popular. . . .'

[6] Letter of 31 March 1808.

[7] Letter to Sir George Beaumont of Jan.–Feb. 1808.

[8] Letter to Sara and Mary Hutchinson, 14 June 1802.

[9] Letter to Lady Beaumont of 21 May 1807. All the other quotations in this paragraph, except the last, come also from this letter.

my Poems depends'. They are the borrowers from the lending-libraries, the buyers in their thousands of the verse-tales of Scott (and they will be, in a few years, of Byron's). They are the writers and followers of the critical Reviews, they are the idle skimmers who 'do not *read* books, they merely snatch a glance at them that they may talk about them'. Their taste has been incurably corrupted: and that means—to Wordsworth who demanded all from his readers, for whom poetry was an activity worth nothing if not worth everything—that means that *they* are corrupted, morally and totally. Such persons can never have 'any genuine enjoyment of poetry', and they are, therefore, 'without love of human nature and reverence for God'. It is fine sweeping nonsense, if one looks at it coolly—these blandly egoistic identifications between a liking for *his* poetry and a taste for any poetry, and between a lack of taste for poetry and a general moral delinquency—yet Wordsworth, on his own terms, could scarcely say less, and he was never the man to be deterred, by humour or modesty or tactfulness, from saying as much as he meant. For he *did* think of his own poems as moral offerings, made to a moral élite, to 'the young and the gracious of every age', to 'men who lead the simplest lives, and those most according to nature'.[10]

The public, then, had failed him: some other source must yield him the disciples whom his nature demanded. He found it, after a few months of brooding, in something which he called 'the People'. 'Remember,' he writes to Sir George Beaumont a propos of 'Peter Bell', 'remember that no Poem of mine will ever be popular ... I say not this in modest disparagement of the Poem [an unnecessary disclaimer], but in sorrow for the sickly taste of the Public in verse. The *People* would love the Poem of Peter Bell, but the *Public* (a very different Being) will never love it.'[11] What is this 'People', thus set in opposition to that tasteless and corrupted 'Public'? He does not define it for Sir George Beaumont's benefit; but a letter a few months later defines it indirectly. He is writing to a friend who had asked his opinions about national education and the reading habits of the common people; he describes the people he knows, the dalesmen of his native Cumberland, who read, he says, very little except the Bible and also 'half-penny Ballads, and penny and two-penny histories, in great abundance', which they buy off wandering pedlars. Then comes a revealing confession. He had 'many a time wished', he says, 'to produce songs, poems, and little histories, that might circulate among other good things in this way, supplanting partly the bad'. And he adds: 'Indeed, some of the Poems which I have published were composed, not without a hope that at some time or other they might answer this purpose.'[12]

One can see now what the 'People' was and where its attraction lay. It was a dream-public—the sort of public that many a self-conscious, minority writer has dreamed of—whose taste was, miraculously, both

---

[10] Letter to John Wilson of June 1802.
[11] Letter of Jan.–Feb. 1808.
[12] Letter to Francis Wrangham of 5 June 1808.

unlettered and correct; it could be reached directly, anonymously, *naturally*, by-passing all the maddening, uncomprehending middlemen of the republic of letters, all the publishers with profits to make and the critics and readers whose pre-conceived notions of poetry queer the pitch for the simple response. It seems a pity that Wordsworth never, in fact, attempted the broadsheet way of distributing his poems; one might then know if 'the People' would really have 'loved' 'Peter Bell' and the rest. But he is right in one way—right in feeling that some of his poems are fitted for broadsheets: especially the short anecdote poems such as 'We are Seven', 'Anecdote for Fathers', 'Simon Lee', 'The Blind Highland Boy', etc. The broad-sheet qualities are simplicity both of language and thought,[13] directness, singleness (one anecdote and one moral per poem): in a word, completeness. Each poem is a small sufficiency. There is a resemblance here to some of Hardy's poems, and perhaps this is a genuinely folk and rustic quality; these poems are like stories told in country pubs, if the teller were a poet. And the broadsheet project, with the motives behind it, looks oddly forward to Tolstoy, the work and aims of whose later years—moral tales in simple language directed at the Russian peasantry—came also from a blend of didactic purpose—'every great poet is a Teacher'—and impatience with the urban, the literary, and the sophisticated.

It may not be without point that these later writers are brought to mind; for though Wordsworth was by no means the first poet to find himself, or feel himself, uncomprehended by the literary world, I believe he was the first to react to that disagreeable discovery in this particular way—a way which became, if not quite standard, at least common form in later times. The malaise he felt in 1807 is recognizably what has become almost an occupational malaise of contemporary poetry; a sense, irritated and bewildered, not exactly that the poet has no public, but that he has lost contact with a public he might have. They are there, somewhere; they would love him did they but know him, could he but find the channel that would reach them. What stands between him and them is a baffling network of 'stock responses' fed (as he sees it) by literary habits outmoded or corrupt. When writers earlier than romanticism found themselves unappreciated by the literary world, the normal response was to hope that the false taste at the moment dominant would be replaced, within the literary world, by a true taste.[14] They appealed from Caesar unto—they hoped—Caesar's successor. They did not decide that the taste of the literary was corrupt *because* they were literary; they did not turn from them to the unliterary. Perhaps such loss of contact was an inevitable accompaniment of

[13] Jeffrey was quite right, though he meant it in disgusted contempt, when he observed that the sources of Wordsworth's diction of simplicity were 'vulgar ballads and plebeian nurseries'.

[14] Wordsworth—characteristic in this of the nineteenth century—hoped that the spread of popular education would do the trick for his poetry. 'As education is extended,' he writes in 1823, writings of his kind 'will find a proportionate increase of readers'.

romanticism—which demands devotees rather than mere readers willing to be entertained, which will make no concessions (for concessions are betrayals), whose typical figure is the defiant, or lonely, or aesthetic individualist. But whether or not romanticism is to be blamed for it, it is clear that Wordsworth has had many followers in this particular direction. Yeats in his later days, writing little ballad-type songs for broadsheet circulation; Auden sighing for the kind of society in which 'light verse' can flourish because poet and public share the same assumptions; Eliot remarking wistfully that any poet would be pleased to think that he filled a function in society as honourable as that of the music-hall comedian—the dream in all is clearly the same.

But of course the ballad-poems of Yeats and Auden are at the opposite pole from genuine popular art; they are highly sophisticated, read and enjoyed only by the literary; and between the actualities of Eliot's poetry and the actualities of the English music-hall the gulf is enormous. Is there, has there ever been, any basis in fact for the dream? How many writers can one find who were neglected by the literary but loved by the simple—and later admitted by the literary? Very few: and those, in some way or other, are special cases. Bunyan is one: *Pilgrim's Progress*, vastly popular from its publication in 1678, was despised or unknown by the cultured until towards the end of the eighteenth century.[15] But Bunyan wrote for a public—the Bible-and-tract-reading nonconformist public of the late seventeenth century—which through socio-political events had become temporarily and totally alienated from the world of polite letters; when, in the eighteenth century, the two came together again, the appeal of *Pilgrim's Progress* was no longer confined to the former. That is not the typical way; it reverses the typical. The common process is that the errors of the ruling literary are corrected not by the unliterary, but by others, a small minority, at first, of others, among the literary—by a clique which forms itself to defend and expound the new writer. So it was with Whitman, desperately anxious (and for reasons not dissimilar from Wordsworth's) to appeal to the People, but in fact ignored or ridiculed by them and first appreciated by a few highly sophisticated English men of letters—by Rossetti and Swinburne among others, his antitheses in all things. So it was with Eliot: Clive Bell's account is a textbook example of the classic way in which a new writer's fame begins, with an almost private circulation among a small group of the well-placed literary:

> If I met Eliot in 1916, it must have been in '17 that I went to Garsington for an Easter party taking with me some ten or dozen copies of the last, and perhaps the first, publication of the Egoist Press, *The Love Song of J. Alfred Prufrock*. Anyone with a taste for research can fix

15 Johnson's praise of it shows the beginning of its emergence into the favour of the lettered. 'His *Pilgrim's Progress* has great merit . . . and it has had the best evidence of its merit, the general and continued approbation of mankind.' (Boswell, 30 April 1773).

the date, for the book, or brochure rather, had just appeared and I distributed my copies hot from the press like so many Good Friday buns. Who were the recipients? Our host and hostess, Philip and Lady Ottoline Morell, of course, Mrs St John Hutchinson, Katherine Mansfield, Aldous Huxley, Middleton Murry, Lytton Strachey perhaps, and, I think, Gertler. Were there others? Maria Balthus for instance (later Mrs Aldous Huxley). I cannot tell: but of this I am sure, it was Katherine Mansfield who read the poem aloud.[16]

And such, ironically, was the fate of Wordsworth himself. What he most disliked was what happened; he and his works became the centre of a small literary cult. The label of the 'Lake Poets' was affixed: the invention of hostile critics, yet not untrue to the reality. How angry, how disappointed, Wordsworth was to find himself taken in this way may be seen by the violence of his reaction to the opening of Jeffrey's review of the *Poems* of 1807. 'In the first sentence of what he has said of my poems he has shewn a gross want of the common feeling of a British Gentleman. . . . If Mr J. continues to play tricks of this kind, let him take care to arm his breech well, for assuredly he runs desperate risque of having it soundly kicked.'[17] Look up that first sentence, and you find what seems harmless enough—'This author is known to belong to a certain brotherhood of poets who have haunted for some years about the Lakes of Cumberland'—but clearly what enraged Wordsworth was that nothing could be farther than that picture from the poet of his ideal, the 'man speaking to men', the poet in harmony with the People. The irony went farther; for Wordsworth was to find himself jeered at by Byron—and not quite undeservedly—for being *too* literary, too remote from the world of common men; and in fact—it surely *is* a matter of fact, not of opinion—the language, thought, and interests of *Don Juan* were far nearer than those of Wordsworth's poetry to a far larger portion of the English people. He was caught in a dilemma from which there was no escape: committed both by his theories and by his real affinities to the convictions that the People were his proper objective and the People's tastes were sound, he found himself in an age when, undeniably, those whom everyone else would call the People were running mad for verse which *he* regarded as at best mediocre (Scott's or Moore's), at worse pernicious (Byron's). There was no escape: except to invent, for his own consolation, a People which never existed.

And the moral for our own times? It is surely that the writer who is genuinely original must accept the doom of originality; he must wait till the leaven has worked through the mass. He reaches the People (if he ever does) *through* the literary, not in spite of them and not without them. The moral is that a self-conscious, deliberate effort to reach the People, made by writers who are in fact sophisticated, writers-with-a-

---

[16] *T. S. Eliot: a Symposium*, 1948.
[17] Letter to Walter Scott of 18 January 1808.

purpose, is bound to fail; for the People—the real people, not the writer's dream—do have one undeniable critical insight—they can smell a highbrow a mile off, and never is the highbrow more easily detected than when he is pretending to be lowbrow. For to turn to the simple is the last refuge of the over-literary; the truly simple, in a healthy society, aspire to be literary themselves. (In an unhealthy society, like our own, they are merely philistine.) It needs unusual literary sophistication—in other words, it needs genuine originality—to perceive that the tastes of the common reader (Wordsworth's 'Public') have become, at a given moment, out of touch or corrupt; therefore only the truly original are likely to want to appeal from that Public to something else; but just because they are original, that something else (Wordsworth's 'People') is likely to find them just as odd as the Public finds them, and the only way in which it will be at all true that the People 'loves' them will be a mystical and not a factual way: a way perceived only by the writers themselves, or by their literary adherents, while the People themselves remain sublimely unaware of what they are told is theirs. A modern example is D. H. Lawrence. There *is* a sense in which it can be truly affirmed that Lawrence's work comes more directly from a native and popular English tradition than does most contemporary English writing; and Lawrence, like Wordsworth, felt nothing but biting contempt for the literary world of his time: but no one can seriously maintain that the miners of Nottinghamshire are, or ever have been, aware that Lawrence was 'their' writer. And since—after Wordsworth, after romanticism— we are all frantically anxious to rediscover our roots and re-establish our traditions, since we must convince ourselves that what *we* write (and not the best-sellers) is really 'in the tradition', really goes back to those happy times (probably mythical) when People and Public were one, so the literary notion of the People, drifting farther and farther from reality, ends up as not much more than an affirmation of what would be desirable. Hence—as Wordsworth found—much heart-searching, some self-deception, and not a little plain nonsense.

'Wordsworth, the Public and the People', *The Sewanee Review*, LXIV, 1956, pp. 71–80.

An Aspect of Wordsworth's Thought: 1793-7

The *Prelude* records that it was during the next year, 1793, that Words-worth began to have fresh insight into the life of nature,

That in life's everyday appearances
I seemed about this period to have sight
Of a new world, a world, too, that was fit
To be transmitted and made visible
To other eyes, as having for its base.
That whence our dignity originates.[1]

This new world entered his poetry for the first time in 1794, in the corrections which he was then making to 'An Evening Walk'.

A heart that vibrates evermore, awake
To feelings for all forms that Life can take,
That wider still its sympathy extends
And sees not any line where being ends;
Sees sense, through Nature's rudest forms betrayed,
Tremble obscure in fountain, rock and shade,
And while a secret power these forms endears
Their social accent never vainly hears.[2]

These lines might epitomize the whole new creed as it had developed in France. Its key words—Nature, life, sense, forms, secret power—are the favourites both of the later *philosophes* and of the mature Words-worth. But the lines differ from the philosophers' speculations in two ways. They describe an emotional experience in which the forms are endeared to the beholder, and these forms speak with a social accent—that is, they have some significance for his life among men. Such significance is characteristic of mystical experiences.[3] The lines seem to be not a statement of theory but a description of the experiences

---

[1] *The Prelude* (1805), XII. 369–74.
[2] *Poetical Works*, ed. E. de Selincourt, i, p. 10. The publication of these additions disposes of the suggestion made by C. Cestre, *La Révolution française et les poètes anglais*, and others, that Coleridge was the source of Wordsworth's ideas on the life in Nature.
[3] See E. Aegerter, *Le Mysticisme*, p. 27.

which Wordsworth had begun to have in 1793, and which were to shape
his interpretation of the doctrine he had met in Paris.

Another of these corrections shows that he was using the word 'forms'
as Robinet and other *philosophes* had used it, to mean organized bodies
of sentient matter. The correction also shows that Wordsworth then
traced his belief in the life of nature more to science than to that fancy
which *The Prelude* gives as the only source.

> And are there souls whose languid powers unite
> No interest to each rural sound or sight. . . .
> How different with those favoured souls who, taught
> By active Fancy or by patient Thought,
> See common forms prolong the endless chain
> Of joy and grief, of pleasure and of pain;
> But chiefly those to whom the harmonious doors
> Of Science have unbarred celestial stores. . . .
> With them the sense no trivial object knows,
> Oft at its meanest touch their spirit glows,
> And proud beyond all limits to aspire
> Mounts through the fields of thought on wings of fire.
> But sure with tenfold pleasure they behold
> The powers of Nature in each various mould,
> If like the Sun their (   ) love surrounds
> The various world to life's remotest bounds,
> Yet not extinguishes the warmer fire
> Round which the close domestic train retire.[4]

In the Associationist philosophy which was popular in England, the
word 'forms' meant those shapes which were perceived as simple ideas,
and it might as well refer to a table as a tree. Clearly, Wordsworth's
'common forms' which 'prolong the endless chain Of joy and grief, of
pleasure and of pain' do not bear this meaning, nor, in the preceding
quotation, do those 'rudest forms' which still possess 'sense' that can
'tremble obscure'. Here 'form' seems to mean any organized natural
body, and the implication is that such bodies have life and sensibility.
This is the sense of the word 'form' which Diderot employed when, to
summarize his belief that every organized body of matter, however
small or apparently inanimate, had its own little degree of feeling and
perception, he wrote that 'every form has the happiness or the un-
happiness which is proper to it', and Robinet was using the word in the
same sense when he postulated that 'material forms' are only produced
by being 'animated' by the 'active power', 'organic living and animal',
which is 'the foundation of the visible world'.[5] Whatever has form in
this sense has organized being, independent life and feeling. To con-

4 *Poetical Works*, i, pp. 12–13.
5 J. B. R. Robinet, *Considerations philosophiques de la gradation naturelles des
formes de l'être*, pp. 5–12.

template the forms is to contemplate their life and that life of the universe of which it is part.

The years 1793 and 1794 seem to have been those in which Wordsworth absorbed the new philosophy of nature and began to apply it to his own experience. It is quite probable that he had experienced moments of ecstasy in his childhood, but he was now, as he had not been before, equipped with a theory which explained them both in religious and scientific terms as a direct contact with the divine principle of the world. This was perhaps the first time that the new philosophy had reached a poet of original mind who was already a lover of natural scenery and steeped in eighteenth-century nature poetry, so it is not surprising that it should be given a less abstract turn. Moreover, at this time, Wordsworth was a lonely man in a world where events stronger than his will had swept the control of his life out of his hands. Reconciliation to life for him meant the contemplation of Necessity and reconciliation with it. He desperately needed to find a religious system in which to believe.

So far, the ideas which he had adopted explained only the moments of ecstasy. They had not been tested by any attempt to explain the miseries of the world, and to those that mourn they had nothing to say. The impulse to work out his ideas thoroughly seems to have come from the contemplation of suffering and despair, and it was in the years when he was

> oppressed by sense
> Of instability, revolt, decay,
> And change and emptiness.[6]

and learned to overcome it, that Wordsworth elaborated his theories into a quasi-religion.

The moods of ecstatic insight which Wordsworth experienced in his solitary wanderings of 1793, were soon succeeded by the despair which followed his brief conversion to Godwinism and his disillusionment with it. In 1795 he tried to analyse the despairing mind in a fragment, 'Incipient Madness', which recounts a visit to a ruined cottage. The mood, as he described it, was marked by a rebellion against the laws of nature, as the other mood had been by sympathy with nature. In short, the two states were those which he would later have described as the imaginative and the fanciful.

> She said: 'that wagon does not care for us'—
> The words were simple, but her look and voice
> Made up their meaning and bespoke a mind
> Which being long neglected, and denied
> The common food of hope, was now become
> Sick and extravagant,—by strong access
> Of momentary pangs driven to that state

6 *The Excursion*, III. 137–9.

In which all past experience melts away,
And the rebellious heart to its own will
Fashions the laws of nature.[7]

The visit to this cottage was an experience to which Wordsworth
returned often in his later thinking; he made it the subject of 'The
Ruined Cottage', and out of material originally written for that poem
grew both *The Prelude* and *The Excursion*. For the moment Wordsworth was content to contrast the two states of mind—despair with its
fanciful attempts to subject nature to the morbid mind, and ecstasy,
subjecting the mind to nature and finding human significance there.
This contrast was the theme of his most successful early poem, 'Lines
left upon a Seat in a Yew-Tree', written in 1795.

> he many an hour
> A morbid pleasure nourished, tracing here
> An emblem of his own unfruitful life:
> And, lifting up his head, he then would gaze
> On the more distant scene,—how lovely 'tis
> Thou seest,—and he would gaze till it became
> Far lovelier, and his heart could not sustain
> The beauty, still more beauteous! Nor, that time,
> When Nature had subdued him to herself,
> Would he forget those Beings to whose minds,
> Warm from the labours of benevolence,
> The world, and human life, appeared a scene
> Of kindred loveliness: then he would sigh,
> Inly disturbed, to think that others felt
> What he must never feel: and so, lost Man!
> On visionary views would Fancy feed
> Till his eye streamed with tears . . .
> If Thou be one whose heart the holy forms
> Of young imagination have kept pure,
> Stranger! henceforth be warned; and know that pride,
> Howe'er disguised in its own majesty,
> Is littleness; that he, who feels contempt
> For any living thing, hath faculties
> Which he has never used.[8]

Thus Wordsworth's experiences had deepened the philosophical speculations on living nature into a belief in the possibility of real contact
with the life in nature—a contact in which the forms of nature made, as
it were, a language. But his experience had taught him also that the
language could be misunderstood—the forms misread—by a rebellious
mind seeking emblems of its own despair. Later, in the Solitary's
description of

[7] 'Incipient Madness', ll. 56–65.
[8] 'Lines left upon a Seat in a Yew-Tree', ll. 30–54.

> a troubled mind:

That, in a struggling and distempered world,
Saw a seductive image of herself,

he suggested that there could seem to be two kinds of nature.

> Here Nature was my guide,

The Nature of the dissolute; but thee,
O fostering Nature! I rejected—smiled
At others tears in pity; and in scorn
At those, which thy soft influence sometimes drew
From my unguarded heart.[9]

But the Solitary was the *advocatus diaboli* of *The Excursion*, or as near as Wordsworth could come to such a figure. Wordsworth himself continued to distinguish the two moods as those of the rebellious spirit and the spirit subdued to Nature.

> A plastic power

Abode with me, a forming hand, at times
Rebellious, acting in a devious mood,
A local spirit of its own, at war
With general tendency, but for the most
Subservient strictly to the external things
With which it communed.[10]

In *The Excursion* he elaborated this to show five different responses to the same natural scene. First the Wanderer describes his response, which is imaginative, recognizing 'a semblance strange of power intelligent' and

Measuring through all degrees, until the scale
Of time and conscious nature disappear,
Lost in unsearchable eternity![11]

Then the Solitary describes two responses, that of the Fancy, 'beguiling harmlessly the listless hours' by tracing humorous resemblances, and that of the same mind oppressed by sense of change and emptiness, when the contemplation feeds 'Pity and scorn and melancholy pride'. He then points out the different response of the botanist or mineralogist and the Wanderer in turn points to the child, 'Dame Nature's pupil of the lowest form'. This careful elaboration is an interesting example of the continuity of Wordsworth's thought, and of its dependence on his earlier experiences.

What Wordsworth meant at this time by the forms of nature and their 'social accents' is less clear, though the subject occupied his mind in the

---

[9] *The Excursion*, III. 808–12.
[10] *The Prelude* (1805), II. 381–7.
[11] *The Excursion*, III. 110–12.

following years. It would seem that he regarded the natural forms as outward and visible expressions of the spiritual force in nature. A fragment written at Alfoxden reads

> And never for each other shall we feel
> As we may feel, till we have sympathy
> With nature in her forms inanimate,
> With objects such as have no power to hold
> Articulate language. In all forms of things
> There is a mind.[12]

The Excursion says the same thing more clearly.

> There is an active principle alive
> In all things, in all natures, in the flowers
> And in the trees
> . . .
> All beings have their properties which spread
> Beyond themselves, a power by which they make
> Some other being conscious of their life,
> Spirit that knows no insulated spot,
> No chasm, no solitude; from link to link
> It circulates, the Soul of all the worlds.[13]

Thus the Spirit makes its life known through the Forms, and the whole doctrine rests on an emotional, and perhaps mystical response to them. When this response is made in submission to Nature, and with a sense of her laws and purposes, then 'an auxiliar light' comes from the mind, adding beauty and human meaning to the landscape.

Wordsworth then had come to some of his most important beliefs long before Coleridge visited Alfoxden in June 1797. Those beliefs had a good deal in common with the ones which Coleridge had reached on his own account. It is interesting that one of the first results of the meeting was a note from Wordsworth to Joseph Cottle, asking the bookseller to send a copy of Darwin's *Zoonomia* post-haste, and telling him that a copy could be borrowed, if necessary, from Tom Wedgwood's library. It is impossible to say which poet was introducing the other to this book, for its doctrine of living force in matter was one which they both believed.

Nevertheless each poet had something to add to the other's theories. Coleridge believed that the influence of nature (and hence of God in nature) worked by education, often involving terror. Following Hartley he believed that the purpose of this education was a knowledge of the divine[14] and that the period of direct influence (until the coming Apo-

---

[12] *Poetical Works*, V. p. 340.

[13] *The Excursion*, IX. 1–15 and app. crit. The lines are quoted in the form they had in MS 18A, written in 1798–9.

[14] 'Religious Musings', ll. 40–4 and note.

calypse) was the childhood of the man or of the race.[15] On the other hand Wordsworth believed in the possibility of direct communion with Nature and of direct insight into her life.

Again, for Coleridge, Nature was symbolical, by which he meant that its appearances were designed to impress the mind of man and to bring him to know God. For Wordsworth the forms of nature were expressive of an independent life which was to be known and loved for its own sake and this love brought with it illumination and benevolence towards all life. The theory which emerged from the discussions between the two poets took account of both sets of views.

The word around which the emerging theory crystallized was Imagination. Each poet had at first rested his views of the natural world chiefly on science. For Wordsworth the 'favoured souls' were

> chiefly those to whom the harmonious doors
> Of science have unbarred celestial stores . . .[16]

while Coleridge's elaborate mathematical arguments in *Joan of Arc* and his attention to Darwin's science and Priestley's experiments have already been noticed. The request for *Zoonomia* would indicate that the scientific basis of their ideas remained but each had also named 'Fancy' as an important agent of knowledge. For Coleridge

> Fancy is the power
> That first unsensualizes the dark mind,[17]

while Wordsworth's favoured soul could be taught

> By active Fancy or by patient Thought,[18]

More recently, in the 'Lines on a Seat in a Yew-Tree' Wordsworth had used the word Imagination to describe the power of true response to Nature and, in doing so, he had brought into the discussion what was already a potent word. Many of the points of Coleridge's later theory are to be found scattered throughout eighteenth-century writings and the imagination had already been described in different places as intuitive, superior to reason, and creative.[19] These suggestions of suprarational power, and also the part which the word played in theories seeking to explain the mind's contact with the external world, made it a very suitable word for all that Wordsworth and Coleridge were now trying to clarify.

From *The Active Universe. Pantheism and the Concept of Imagination in the English Romantic Poets*, University of London: Athlone Press, 1962, pp. 72–80.

[15] 'The Destiny of Nations', ll. 18–23 and app. crit., 77–86; 'Religious Musings', ll. 208–12.

[16] *Poetical Works*, ed. E. de Selincourt, I. pp. 12–13 app. crit.

[17] *The Destiny of Nations*, ll. 80–1.

[18] *Poetical Works*, I. pp. 12–13.

[19] Wilma L. Kennedy, *The English Heritage of Coleridge of Bristol*, pp. 91–2

The Old Cumberland Beggar

'The Old Cumberland Beggar' (1797) is Wordsworth's finest vision of the irreducible natural man, the human stripped to the nakedness of primordial condition and exposed as still powerful in dignity, still infinite in value. The Beggar reminds us of the beggars, solitaries, wanderers throughout Wordsworth's poetry, particularly in *The Prelude* and 'Resolution and Independence'. He differs from them in that he is not the agency of a revelation; he is not responsible for a sudden release of Wordsworth's imagination. He is not even of visionary utility; he is something finer, beyond use, a vision of reality in himself. I am not suggesting that 'The Old Cumberland Beggar' is the best of Wordsworth's poems outside *The Prelude*; it is not in the sublime mode, as are 'Tintern Abbey', the Great Ode, 'Resolution and Independence'. But it is the most Wordsworthian of poems, and profoundly moving.

Nothing could be simpler than the poem's opening: 'I saw an aged Beggar in my walk.' The Old Man (the capitalization is the poet's) has put down his staff, and takes his scraps and fragments out of a flour bag, one by one. He scans them, fixedly and seriously. The plain beginning yields to a music of love, the beauty of the real:

> In the sun,
> Upon the second step of that small pile,
> Surrounded by those wild unpeopled hills,
> He sat, and ate his food in solitude:
> And ever, scattered from his palsied hand,
> That, still attempting to prevent the waste,
> Was baffled still, the crumbs in little showers
> Fell on the ground; and the small mountain birds,
> Not venturing yet to peck their destined meal,
> Approached within the length of half his staff

It is difficult to describe *how* this is beautiful, but we can make a start by observing that it is beautiful both because it is so matter of fact, and because the fact is itself a transfiguration. The Old Man is in his own state, and he is radically innocent. The 'wild unpeopled hills' complement his own solitude; he is a phenomenon of their kind. And he is no more sentimentalized than they are. His lot is not even miserable; he is too absorbed into nature for that, as absorbed as he can be and still retain human identity.

He is even past further ageing. The poet has known him since his childhood, and even then 'he was so old, he seems not older now'. The Old Man is so helpless in appearance that everyone—sauntering horseman or toll-gate keeper or post boy—makes way for him, taking special care to keep him from harm. For he cannot be diverted, but moves on like a natural process. 'He travels on, a solitary Man,' Wordsworth says, and then repeats it, making a refrain for that incessant movement whose only meaning is that it remains human though at the edge of our condition:

> He travels on, a solitary Man;
> His age has no companion. On the ground
> His eyes are turned, and, as he moves along,
> They move along the ground; and, evermore,
> Instead of common and habitual sight
> Of fields with rural works, of hill and dale,
> And the blue sky, one little span of earth
> Is all his prospect.

He is bent double, like the Leech Gatherer, and his vision of one little span of earth recalls the wandering old man of Chaucer's 'Pardoner's Tale'. But Chaucer's solitary longed for death, and on the ground he called his mother's gate he knocked often with his staff, crying 'Dear mother, let me in'. Wordsworth's Old Man sees only the ground, but he is tenaciously alive, and is beyond desire, even that of death. He sees, and yet hardly sees. He moves constantly, but is so still in look and motion that he can hardly be seen to move. He is all process, hardly character, and yet almost stasis.

It is so extreme a picture that we can be tempted to ask, 'Is this life? Where is its use?' The temptation dehumanizes us, Wordsworth would have it, and the two questions are radically dissimilar, but his answer to the first is vehemently affirmative and to the second an absolute moral passion. There is:

> a spirit and pulse of good,
> A life and soul, to every mode of being
> Inseparably linked.

The Old Man performs many functions. The most important is that of a binding agent for the memories of good impulses in all around him. Wherever he goes:

> The mild necessity of use compels
> To acts of love.

These acts of love, added one to another, at last insensibly dispose their performers to virtue and true goodness. We need to be careful in our reaction to this. Wordsworth is not preaching the vicious and mad doctrine that beggary is good because it makes charity possible. That would properly invoke Blake's blistering reply in 'The Human Abstract':

> Pity would be no more
> If we did not make somebody Poor;
> And Mercy no more could be
> If all were as happy as we.

Wordsworth has no reaction to the Old Man which we can categorize. He does not think of him in social or economic terms, but only as a human life, which necessarily has affected other lives, and always for the better. In particular, the Old Man has given occasions for kindness to the very poorest, who give to him from their scant store, and are the kinder for it. Again, you must read this in its own context. Wordsworth's best poetry has nothing directly to do with social justice, as Blake's or Shelley's frequently does. The old beggar is a free man, at home in the heart of the solitudes he wanders, and he does not intend the humanizing good he passively causes. Nor is his social aspect at the poem's vital centre; only his freedom is:

> —Then let him pass, a blessing on his head!
> And, long as he can wander, let him breathe
> The freshness of the valleys; let his blood
> Struggle with frosty air and winter snows;
> And let the chartered wind that sweeps the heath
> Beat his grey locks against his withered face.

Pity for him is inappropriate; he is pathetic only if shut up. He is a 'figure of capable imagination', in Stevens' phrase, a Man perfectly complete in Nature, reciprocating its gifts by being himself, a being at one with it:

> Let him be free of mountain solitudes;
> And have around him, whether heard or not,
> The pleasant melody of woodland birds.

Mountain solitudes and sudden winds are what suit him, whether he react to them or not. The failure of his senses does not cut him off from nature; it does not matter whether he can hear the birds, but it is fitting that he have them around him. He has become utterly passive towards nature. Let it be free, then, to come in upon him:

> if his eyes have now
> Been doomed so long to settle upon earth
> That not without some effort they behold
> The countenance of the horizontal sun,
> Rising or setting, let the light at least
> Find a free entrance to their languid orbs.

The Old Man is approaching that identity with nature that the infant at first knows, when an organic continuity seems to exist between nature and consciousness. Being so naturalized, he must die in the eye of nature, that he may be absorbed again:

> And let him, *where* and *when* he will, sit down
> Beneath the trees, or on a grassy bank
> Of highway side, and with the little birds
> Share his chance-gathered meal; and, finally,
> As in the eye of Nature he has lived,
> So in the eye of Nature let him die!

The poem abounds in a temper of spirit that Wordsworth shares with Tolstoy, a reverence for the simplicities of *caritas*, the Christian love that is so allied to and yet is not pity. But Tolstoy might have shown the Old Cumberland Beggar as a sufferer; in Wordsworth he bears the mark of 'animal tranquillity and decay', the title given by Wordsworth to a fragment closely connected to the longer poem. In the fragment the Old Man travels on and moves not with pain, but with thought:

> He is insensibly subdued
> To settled quiet . . .
> He is by nature led
> To peace so perfect that the young behold
> With envy, what the Old Man hardly feels.

We know today, better than his contemporaries could, what led Wordsworth to the subject of human decay, to depictions of idiocy, desertion, beggars, homeless wanderers. He sought images of alienated life, as we might judge them, which he could see and present as images of natural communion. The natural man, free of consciousness in any of our senses, yet demonstrates a mode of consciousness which both intends nature for its object and at length blends into that object. The hiding places of man's power are in his past, in childhood. Only memory can take him there, but even memory fades, and at length fades away. The poet of naturalism, separated by organic growth from his own past, looks around him and sees the moving emblems of a childlike consciousness in the mad, the outcast, and the dreadfully old. From them he takes his most desperate consolation, intimations of a mortality that almost ceases to afflict.

From 'William Wordsworth', *The Visionary Company*, London: Faber and Faber, 1962, pp. 120–93 (173–8).

ALBERT S. GÉRARD

Exploring *Tintern Abbey*

'Tintern Abbey' shares with Coleridge's 'The Eolian Harp' the dubious honour of being one of the most lopsidedly quoted poems in the whole corpus of English Romantic poetry. No student of Wordsworth, or, for that matter, of Romanticism in general, can refrain from squeezing all the doctrinal juice he can out of lines 35-49 and 93-111. Those two passages are admittedly remarkable for the loftiness of the feelings and ideas they convey, and for the eloquence with which they are conveyed. In consequence it is hard to resist the temptation of extending to the poem as a whole the triumphant impression they make on the reader. Thus we find F. W. Bateson confidently asserting of 'Tintern Abbey' that 'rhetorically it is superbly assured and persuasive'.[1] This is probably the reason why it was so dear to Victorian hearts. But the present age feels only contemptuous dislike for what is 'superbly assured': hence the twentieth-century reaction against 'Tintern Abbey'. For F. W. Bateson, the poem 'conceals a confession of failure'. For William Empson, it is a hopeless muddle on all planes, beginning with the grammatical. For G. H. Hartman, Wordsworth's purpose in it was 'to convey a disproportion between his high feelings and the visible character of the scene'.[2] 'Tintern Abbey' is obviously an important and a complex poem, and only a close analysis of its structure is likely to reveal its total meaning by bringing out the significance of each part in relation to the whole.

Stanza I raises a problem with which I have dealt at length elsewhere,[3] namely whether there is a connection between the Wye landscape and the cluster of memories and speculations which constitute the body of the poem. Close reading indicates that the landscape is truly symbolic in Coleridge's sense of the term, i.e., that it is both naturalistic and significant. It contains the elements which are going to constitute the general pattern of the poem. In its insistence that the setting Wordsworth is describing is a revisited landscape, it anticipates the intricate weaving of the themes of time and memory, which are necessarily

---

[1] F. W. Bateson, *Wordsworth: A Re-interpretation* (London, 1954), p. 142.
[2] Geoffrey H. Hartman, *The Unmediated Vision* (New Haven, 1954), p. 7.
[3] Albert Gérard, 'Symbolic Landscape in Wordsworth's "Tintern Abbey"', *Publications de l'Université de l'État à Élisabethville*, IV (Dec. 1962), 21-30. See also James Benziger, '"Tintern Abbey" Revisited', *PMLA*, LXV (1950), 154-162.

central to Wordsworth's deep preoccupation with the growth of the mind. In its indirect references to the three planes of being (the natural, the human, and the divine), it adumbrates the great Romantic vision of cosmic unity. The upward movement of the cliffs and the smoke prepares the reader's mind for the recurring pattern of ascent towards spiritual insight which dominates the structure of the poem.

Nor is the relationship between the Wye landscape and the poem symbolical only. It is also causal. Because of its actual objective features which, as perceived by Wordsworth, become what Coleridge would call 'rays of intellect',[4] it is natural that the Tintern landscape should have started, in the poet's mind, the ruminative process of which the poem is the record; it is natural that a revisited landscape should prompt him to reflections on his own inner development; it is equally natural that the quiet harmony of the landscape should lead him to think of the cosmic unity of Being and, by contrast, of his own inner perplexities, which he is endeavouring to define.

In this latter respect, we must observe that the landscape description of stanza I is far less purely objective than might be thought on a superficial reading. The strong sensory assertions ('I hear', 'I behold', 'I see') unexpectedly lead to the somewhat dubious statement that the smoke—which the poet does see—gives

> some *uncertain* notice, *as might seem,*
> Of vagrant dwellers in the houseless woods,
> Or of some Hermit's cave, where by his fire
> The Hermit sits alone.[5]

In a way, this intimation of human presence brings the landscape description to a climax. Admittedly, as F. W. Bateson rightly comments, 'hermits were one of the conventional properties of late eighteenth-century landscape, and their presence guaranteed the aesthetic, non-documentary quality of the picture'. So were gypsies. But thinking back on the beggar woman in 'An Evening Walk', on 'The Female Vagrant', on 'The Mad Mother', we remember what Mary Moorman has called Wordsworth's 'natural attraction to the ragged vagrant',[6] which lifts the motif above the level of mere literary convention and turns the character into an emblem of suffering mankind. Within the framework of the poem, the vagrants announce 'the still, sad music of humanity'. And as we remember 'The Old Cumberland Beggar' or 'Resolution and Independence', it becomes clear that Wordsworth has endowed the conventional eighteenth-century hermit with a significance that goes beyond the mere picturesque: his solitaries exemplify the highest form of contemplation and wisdom; they are man stripped of all inessentials,

---

[4] 'On Poesy or Art' in *Biographia Literaria*, ed. J. Shawcross (Oxford, 1907), II, 258.

[5] The italics are mine.

[6] Mary Moorman, *William Wordsworth, A Biography, The Early Years: 1770–1803* (Oxford, 1957), p. 118.

living in intimate communion with nature.[7] Thus the Hermit in his cave carries a faint suggestion of the human ideal towards which Wordsworth was groping at the time, and which he was to define with greater assurance in later poems.

But seen from a different angle, this late intrusion of man into the natural landscape, has an anticlimactic effect, thus setting a pattern which, as I hope to make clear, recurs throughout the poem. It is not only that the half-conventional figures of the vagrants and the hermit suggest some slackening of the poetic tension initially created by the immediate sensory presence of the natural scenery. What must be stressed is that the poet shows himself conscious that he is passing from objective data to subjective inference (as is shown by the italicized words in the above quotation), which entails a corresponding loosening of his grasp on the actual. There is, then, already in stanza I, an implicit contrast between what is observed and what is imagined, between fact and hypothesis, which is fundamental to the poem as a whole and prepares for the deeper perplexity to which Wordsworth is about to turn his attention.

Stanza II deals with the interval between Wordsworth's two visits to the place and the effect of his remembrance of 'these beauteous forms' on his mind. After the introduction, it is divided into two sentences, both of which begin with the verb 'owe'. As Wordsworth turns from an objective-symbolical description of external nature to an analysis of his inner self, nature appears as the main causal factor in his moral evolution.

Although the constant use of run-on lines creates an impression of smooth continuousness and organic unity, the stanza has a strong structure, both grammatical and thematic. The two sentences are different in the tone and the nature of the statements they make. The first sentence deals with two 'gifts',—'sensations' and 'feelings'—which are presented as undoubtedly originating in nature. It also deals with the psychological and moral consequences of those gifts: in the first case, the 'sensations sweet' have wrought a 'tranquil restoration' of the poet's 'pure₁ mind'; in the second, a note of diffidence creeps in as Wordsworth passes from the psychological to the moral plane: his 'feelings of unremembered pleasure' have '*perhaps*' led him to 'acts of kindness and of love'. There is thus a gradual ascent from the sensory to the psychological and the moral; on the other hand, slight undertones of doubt are introduced in the passage from the psychological to the ethical.

This pattern is reproduced and developed in the second sentence: besides the sensations and the feelings, Wordsworth's recollections of

[7] On Wordsworth's solitaries, see John Jones, *The Egotistical Sublime: A History of Wordsworth's Imagination* (London, 1954), pp. 61–70, and A. S. Gérard, ' "Resolution and Independence": Wordsworth's Coming of Age', *English Studies in Africa*, III (1960), 8–20.

nature have also kindled in him a 'blessed *mood*'; this mood is described as such at great length and with considerable eloquence. But in the last line a new element is introduced, parallel to the 'tranquil restoration' and the 'acts of kindness' of the first stanza in the same way as the mood itself parallels the 'sensations' and the 'feelings': the blessed mood is interpreted as a mystical insight into the life of things.

Apart from the iterative patterning, a comparison between both parts of the stanza reveals a threefold change in the tone and subject matter: first, a raising of the level of reminiscence, which now passes from the ethical to the mystical; second, a heightened poetic intensity which makes the passage particularly memorable and eminently quotable; third, an increase in the note of diffidence, exemplified by the words 'I trust' and 'may'.

These last two qualities may sound contradictory, yet they are equally important for a balanced understanding of the poem and they provide the key to its meandering structure. For 'Tintern Abbey' is built on a pattern of ascent and descent which is repeated twice: ascent towards the lofty heights of mystical speculation, descent towards the firm ground of ascertained fact. The poetic—we might even say, vatic—quality of lines 37–49 shows how profoundly moving such mystical thoughts were to Wordsworth. But they are only one source of his inspiration. The other is provided by his experience of the actual, the matter-of-fact. If Wordsworth is probably the most impressive and complete impersonation of the Romantic spirit, he owes it to this dual character. While stressing the contradictory aspects of Wordsworth's 'two voices', F. W. Bateson acknowledges that 'in his most characteristic poems, like "Resolution and Independence" . . . the Two Voices turn out to be complementary instead of being contradictory'.[8] It belongs to the essence of Romanticism that it should aim at the reconciliation of opposite elements, and in no other Romantic poet (with the possible exception of Keats) was the duality of realism and idealism so strongly marked as in Wordsworth. This circumstance implies that Wordsworth was fully aware (as Coleridge reminded him) of the somewhat pedestrian character of his matter-of-fact, down-to-earth inspiration; but he was equally aware of the subjective, hypothetical, unascertainable character of his mystical inspiration. His great achievement is that he became able, at times, to reconcile both; but we cannot emphasize too strongly that that stage was not yet in sight when he wrote 'Tintern Abbey'. In this poem, we can see his mind at work during a transitional period: taking his cue from the very objective landscape (stanza I), he works his way through equally matter-of-fact psychological experiences up to dizzy heights of mystical speculation (stanza II). But the more he rises above his actual sensory and psychological experience, the less assured he is of the truth of his speculations: hence the return, in stanza III, to less sublime but more factual considerations.

[8] Bateson, op. cit., p. 4.

Norman Lacey is one of the few critics who have felt the need to see the sublime passage of stanza II in the context of the whole poem. He is thus driven to point out, speaking of the passage from stanza II to stanza III, that Wordsworth 'is not certain what kind of connection there is, if any, between nature and his mystical experience, and he returns to what he knows for certain, that in the fret and fever of the world he has often turned for relief to his memory of the beautiful scene in the Wye valley'.[9]

In fact, Wordsworth's doubt bears on two entirely different points: in the first place, as Lacey says, he is not quite sure that his 'blessed mood' is actually due to the influence of the 'beauteous forms' of nature; although the mood itself is an uncontrovertible psychological fact, its origin is not quite clear. On the other hand, a far stronger doubt is cast on what might be called the cognitive content Wordsworth is tempted to assign to the mood. 'This' in line 49 refers to what immediately precedes, i.e., the suggestion that 'we see into the life of things': it is the interpretation of the mood which Wordsworth concedes may be 'but a vain belief'.

It is essential to the so often unrecognized pathos of 'Tintern Abbey' that as the poet soars to ever loftier heights of speculation, he feels the more in danger of losing his grasp upon the actual, which provided his initial inspiration. That is the reason why, in stanza III, Wordsworth falls back on the matter of ascertained inner experience which formed the starting-point of stanza II: the relief wrought in him by the memory of the Wye amidst 'the fretful stir unprofitable, and the fever of the world'—a phrase which simply enlarges on the 'din of towns and cities'. Stanza III gives a definite sense of anticlimax. But this is no blemish on the poem as a whole. The anticlimax is inherent in the subject matter of the poem, which deals with the alternate moods through which Wordsworth passes as he tentatively gropes after the meanings both certain and possible of his experience of nature.

Coming to stanza IV, we briefly revert to the present of stanza I ('And now . . .'), only to be referred to a slightly remoter past than in stanza II. While the poet, in stanza II, analyses the effect of Nature's 'beauteous forms' during the interval between his two visits to Tintern Abbey, in stanza IV he begins by trying to recapture his mood at the time of his first visit. Since he even mentions his 'boyish days', the stanza deals with three moments in time which are neatly homologous with the three aspects of nature's effects in stanza II: there is an unobtrusive correspondence between the 'sensations', the 'feelings', and the 'gift of aspect more sublime' of stanza II on the one hand, and the 'glad animal movements', the 'passion', and the 'other gifts' of stanza IV on the other.

The introductory lines of stanza IV are of considerable interest in that

[9] *Wordsworth's View of Nature* (Cambridge, 1948), p. 3; the same idea is also expressed on p. 63.

they show the poet aware of the complexity of his mood. 'Perplexity' is probably the key word to the total meaning of the poem. And Wordsworth's puzzlement is the result of two main causes. In what precedes, there is ample evidence of an uncertainty which, as has been said, bears on two important points. But his puzzlement is not of a merely intellectual order. His 'sad perplexity' anticipates another kind of uncertainty, which is the subject of stanza IV and which is concerned with his valuation of the changes—the losses and the new gifts—which time has wrought in him. In those introductory lines, past, present, and future are closely correlated; so are sadness and pleasure. The reason for the sadness and the perplexity is the plain fact that his 'pleasing thoughts/ That in this moment there is life and food/For future years', although deduced from past experience, are less assured than the tranquil, self-possessed phrasing might suggest: they are not more than a 'hope' which the poet 'dares' to entertain. Consequently, in order to disentangle the threads woven into his complex and contradictory mood, Wordsworth is driven to try a new approach by tracing back the main trend of his own evolution.

As Campbell and Mueschke have observed, the poem develops through a process of 'incremental repetition'.[10] In a sustained endeavour to assess his present relationship to nature, Wordsworth first analyses the influence which the memory of the Wye landscape has exerted upon his mind (stanza II); he thus reaches the idea of a glorious mystical insight, the truth of which, however, remains doubtful in his own eyes. He then tackles the problem from another angle and retraces his own evolution from boyhood to maturity, thus encompassing a far wider stretch of time in stanza IV than in stanza II: this retracing is part of the incremental aspect of the process.

Its repetitive aspect is obvious. As the poet contrasts what he is with what he was, we again notice the three-stage ascending trend already perceived in stanza II: from the 'glad animal movements' of his boyhood through the passionate love of natural forms characteristic of his youth to the more thoughtful attitude of his early maturity. But in this respect too the repetition is incremental: the ascending movement, we might say, takes us higher up in stanza IV than in stanza II. It takes us to a more sweeping vision of cosmic unity. In the former passage, the poet merely sees 'into the life of *things*'; in the latter, man is included in his vision and the life of things is seen to reside in an all-pervading presence, which is described in grandiose terms with an animistic or pantheistic slant.

In the last dozen lines of stanza IV Wordsworth epitomizes the three aspects of the grand vision that is inspiring him, i.e., (a) his mystical sense of the unity that brings together the multifarious forms of the cosmos ('*all* thinking things, *all* objects of *all* thought'), (b) his con-

---

[10] O. J. Campbell and P. Mueschke, 'Wordsworth's Aesthetic Development, 1795–1802', *Essays and Studies in English and Comparative Literature*, University of Michigan Publications, Language and Literature, X (Ann Arbor, 1933), p. 32.

viction that the source of man's moral and spiritual growth is to be found in all the external forms of nature ('*all* that we behold', '*all* the mighty world of eye, and ear'), and (c) his correlative assurance that nature acts upon the whole of man's personality ('sense', 'thoughts', 'heart', 'soul', 'moral being').

The important point is that the two lines of approach—the static-analytical line of stanza II and the dynamic-biographical line of stanza IV—are convergent. In both cases the main movement carries the poet from the sensory to the emotional and the mystical, from matter-of-fact observation (sensory and psychological) to mystical insight and cosmic vision. This main trend in the rhythmic pattern of the poem is, as we know, truly prophetic of Wordsworth's future development.

But in 1798 this development was by no means obvious to Wordsworth himself, whose genuine perplexity is poetically revealed by the fact that the ascending movement is counteracted at each stage by a descending trend which leads from assurance to uncertainty. The cosmic vision of unity in stanza IV, like the animistic insight of stanza II, while expressed in lines of great eloquence and convincing beauty, is embedded in a strikingly tentative context.

The note of diffidence creeps in, of course, in low-tension passages which are seldom quoted; but when due attention is paid to such phrases as 'so I dare to hope' (l. 65) or 'I would believe' (l. 87), the nature of Wordsworth's perplexity is clarified and its centrality to the poem becomes obvious. His return to Tintern Abbey has reconstructed the externals of the situation that was his five years before; his own inner experience appears all the more different because of the similarity in the setting. These two elements, similitude and difference, are basic and cut across the divisions of outward experience and inner feeling; in spite of the changes wrought in him in the course of the intervening years, one element of his inner experience remains constant: it is to nature that he owes what he has and what he is; the 'aching joys' and 'dizzy raptures' of his youth were gifts of nature; so were the 'tranquil restoration' of his mind and his 'little acts of kindness and of love' in the intervening years; so are the 'serene and blessed mood' and the 'sense sublime' of his present early manhood. But while this 'mood' and this 'sense' and the happiness they induce in him are sheer psychological facts, the value of their content is by no means a matter of certainty. We cannot help remembering at this point that Coleridge, in 'The Eolian Harp', dismisses as 'shapings of the unregenerate mind' a similarly glorious vision (with a similarly pantheistic tinge) of the One Life.[11]

The beginning of stanza V—'Nor perchance, | If I were not thus

[11] See A. S. Gérard, 'Counterfeiting Infinity: "The Eolian Harp" and the Growth of Coleridge's Mind', *Journal of English and Germanic Philology*, LX (1961), 411–22; 'The Systolic Rhythm: The Structure of Coleridge's Conversation Poems', *Essays in Criticism*, X (1960), 307–19.

taught',—closely parallels the negative hypothesis of stanza III, thus ushering in a second descending movement leading to a new apparent anticlimax. But this time, it would seem, Wordsworth contemplates a deprivation more fundamental than was the case in the earlier passage. The wording and the structure of stanzas II and III are such as to intimate some diffidence on the part of Wordsworth as to the connection between the 'beauteous forms' and the 'blessed mood' as well as about the mystical significance attributed to the 'blessed mood'. But now Wordsworth prophetically puts forward the far more disquieting suggestion that he might become completely cut off from nature, that he might no longer be taught by nature and the language of the sense. As J. F. Danby has observed, 'the ecstatic harmony is only a phase in a larger movement that passes on, in individual experience, to eventual loss ... Wordsworth had had the most Nature could give, and the more, therefore, it could take away. He includes the record of the high experience in his poem but is aware of the inevitability of loss.'[12] And once again he falls back on a matter of ascertained fact, as he had done in stanza III. The sudden turning to Dorothy, who has not yet been mentioned in the poem, may sound unexpected; yet it fits perfectly into the whole scheme which, as should be clear by now, pulsates between the two poles of Wordsworth's inspiration: the matter-of-fact objectivity of his perception of nature (stanza I), the deep certainty of his own psychological experience (stanza III) and the equally objective and comforting presence of his sister (stanza V) on the one hand, and his lofty but subjective aspiration to insight into the life of things (stanza II) and to an intuition of the unity of the cosmos (stanza IV) on the other. This symmetrical pattern with its alternating rhythm of ascent towards uncommon heights of mystical speculation and descent to the bedrock of sensory and psychological certainty is fundamental to the total meaning of the poem.

For the address to Dorothy is an indirect way for Wordsworth to turn back to his own self and such assurance as he may have gained so far. Indeed, the last stanza repeats, on a smaller scale, the ambitious time scheme of the whole poem. In his sister's present (ll. 116-9 and 134-7), Wordsworth relives his own past as re-created in stanza IV. The imaginary landscape which surrounds Dorothy, with its 'misty mountain winds' is reminiscent of the picturesque presentation of nature in stanza IV rather than of the quiet harmony of stanza I; likewise, Dorothy's 'wild eyes' and 'wild ecstasies' recall her brother's past 'aching joys' and 'dizzy raptures' rather than his present soberly meditative mood. The identification is pushed so far that Wordsworth projects his own present into his sister's future (ll. 137-146): not only will her mood be one of sober pleasure, but her memory of nature will play the same restoring role that is assigned to it in very similar terms in the beginning of stanza II and in stanza III; 'lovely forms' (l. 140) and

[12] J. F. Danby, *The Simple Wordsworth. Studies in the Poems, 1797–1807* (London, 1960), pp. 94–6.

'all sweet sounds and harmonies' (l. 142) echo with significant precision the 'beauteous forms' (l. 23) and the 'sensations sweet' (l. 27) of stanza II; they will provide 'healing thoughts' (l. 144)—analogous to the 'tranquil restoration' (l. 30)—to which she will be able to turn in times of 'solitude, or fear, or pain, or grief' (l. 143) in the same way as her brother now turns to his recollections of natural beauty for solace 'in lonely rooms', and 'mid the din of towns and cities' (ll. 25–6), in 'hours of weariness' (l. 27), when oppressed by 'the fretful stir unprofitable, and the fever of the world' (ll. 52–3).

Dorothy is thus presented as a sort of duplication of her brother, and the close correspondence of their characters and interests and sensibilities may do much to account for the feeling that existed between them. But while, in turning to his sister, Wordsworth is in fact turning imaginatively to his own self and experience, there is, in his anticipation of Dorothy's future as identical with his present, an omission which, so far as I know, has passed unnoticed and is both puzzling and significant.

There is hardly a line in the last stanza which does not refer to some earlier passage. But it contains nothing that might be considered as echoing those parts of the poem where, clearly, Wordsworth's poetic power is at its most intense: the end of stanza II and of stanza IV. Nor is there any reference in it to 'acts of kindness and of love' or to 'the still sad music of humanity'; indeed, human society is evoked in negative terms (ll. 128–31) strongly reminiscent of the first part of stanza II and of stanza III. In other words, all the elements which, in the poem, carry with them overtones, however slight, of diffidence or uncertainty, are left out of the concluding stanza. And the last description of Nature's benevolence (ll. 122–34) is couched in terms as general as those of stanza III.

The quiet, assertive tone of stanza V is unmistakable; yet it is also undeniable that this stanza is keyed at a lower pitch of imaginative thinking than the sublime passages of stanzas II and IV. The poem, therefore, paradoxically ends on a note of assertion which produces a sense of anticlimax. Yet, in this paradox there is no such contradiction as mars 'The Eolian Harp'. For the two contrasting movements are fused into the aesthetic unity of the rhythmic pattern. If, starting from its structural organization, we seek to define the highly complex mood of the poem, we shall find that it is one of perplexity on a background of absolute certainty. The certainty refers to Wordsworth's actual experience of nature as a thing of beauty and a source of healing thoughts; it is characteristic of Wordsworth's honesty, of his determined refusal to sacrifice truth to rhetoric, that he should conclude his poem on a note of lesser sublimity.

But the dynamic nucleus which gives the poem its impetus is of course perplexity. Wordsworth had reached the age when a man pauses to reckon up his losses and his gains for the first time. What his losses were was quite clear to him: he had lost the intimate emotional relationship with nature that was his five years before. The gains were less obvious, for the 'other gifts' twice mentioned in the poem are of a less ascertainable nature, dealing as they do with metaphysical intuitions. Twice in the course of the poem, Wordsworth's inspiration gathers force and soars to mystical heights. But although his poetic eloquence testifies to the intensity of the accompanying emotion, Wordsworth's intellectual honesty prevents him from presenting as fact what is only conjectural. Hence the perplexity. For if the 'other gifts' are but vain belief, the loss, obviously, is total and irrecoverable.

It seems that the painstaking procedures of close textual analysis do little more than confirm Keats's flash of sympathetic insight in a passage which it is necessary to quote in full:

I compare human life to a large Mansion of Many Apartments, two of which I can only describe, the doors of the rest being as yet shut upon me—The first we step into we call the infant or thoughtless Chamber, in which we remain as long as we do not think—We remain there a long while, and notwithstanding the doors of the second Chamber remain wide open, showing a bright appearance, we care not to hasten to it; but are at length imperceptibly impelled by the awakening of the thinking principle—within us— we no sooner get into the second Chamber, which I shall call the Chamber of Maiden-Thought, than we become intoxicated with the light and the atmosphere, we see nothing but pleasant wonders, and think of delaying there for ever in delight: However among the effects this breathing is father of is that tremendous one of sharpening one's vision into the heart and nature of Man—of convincing one's nerves that the World is full of Misery and Heartbreak, Pain, Sickness and oppression—whereby This Chamber of Maiden Thought becomes gradually darken'd and at the same time on all sides of it many doors are set open—but all dark—all leading to dark passages—We see not the ballance of good and evil. We are in a Mist—*We* are now in that state—We feel the 'burden of the Mystery', To this point was Wordsworth come, as far as I can conceive when he wrote 'Tintern Abbey' and it seems to me that his Genius is explorative of those dark Passages.[13]

Yet, there is something that should be added to Keats's observation. For as we reread the first lines of stanza V—'Nor perchance,/If I were not thus taught, *should I the more/Suffer my genial spirits to decay*'—we are struck by a note that anticipates later stages in the poet's development. The way the sentence is turned is suggestive of Wordsworth's stern determination—while contemplating his greatest loss— not to give himself up to the annihilating power of his sad perplexity. Faced with a vital dilemma—either to lose his grasp of the actual, or to admit the vanity of his highest intuitions—it is by an act of the will

[13] *The Letters of John Keats*, ed. Hyder Edward Rollins (Cambridge, 1958), I, 280–1.

based on certain knowledge that Wordsworth decides to seek the meaning which his experience, past and present, holds for the future.

Norman Lacey has expressed his surprise that Wordsworth 'did not realize clearly that he was most certainly in possession of the truth when he was "*laid asleep in body*"—in other words, that his mystical experiences were the only starting point for all true insight "into the life of things", and that he must at all costs pin his faith to *them*, and not to the language of the sense'.[14] There may be some truth in this view, although the symbolic significance inherent in the Wye landscape as perceived by the poet's senses does point to intimations of a living cosmic unity. But the fact remains that we find no attempt, within the poem, at reconciling insight and sensation *on the ideational level*. Nor is there, we must note, any explicit condemnation of the nearly pantheistic utterances of the sublime passages, as we find in Coleridge's 'The Eolian Harp'. This is conclusive proof that Wordsworth was not concerned with offering the final poetic statement of a fully-formed philosophical view of life and the universe, unlike Coleridge, who, as Keats knew, was 'incapable of remaining content with half knowledge'.[15] Wordsworth was first and foremost concerned with expressing the complex totality of a mood which included both elements of knowledge and of half-knowledge.

To knowledge belong his sensory apprehension of nature, the healing power of his memory of nature, his past and Dorothy's present emotional involvement in nature. To half-knowledge belong his speculations on the actual content of his mystical moods and the relationship of these moods with nature, and his perplexity regarding the balance of loss and gain in his own evolution. This division accounts for the dialectical oscillation which drives Wordsworth to statements of sublimity only to stress their hypothetical character immediately afterwards.

But while the dominating mood of the greater part of 'Tintern Abbey' is one of perplexity, it was not in the nature of Wordsworth to rest satisfied with a depiction, however accurate and subtle, of his ambiguous predicament at the moment of writing. Indeed, this ambiguity was something that he wanted to overcome. His final concern, therefore, was with finding, in the lessons of the past and the present, some experiential certainty that might put his mind to rest by supplying a firm basis for his future development. What emerges at the outset of a reflective process remarkable both for its honesty and its profundity, is the confidence expressed in the lines 'Knowing that Nature never did betray/The heart that loved her', where the verb 'knowing' carries the full force of absolute conviction. This certainty, this complete assurance of the benevolence of nature, which is the uncontrovertible conclusion to be drawn from his past, is also the foundation for his 'hope' and his 'trust' and his determination to uphold his 'genial spirits' and his 'cheerful faith'. In which direction the will based on such knowledge is

[14] Lacey, pp. 64–5.
[15] *Letters of John Keats*, I, 194.

going to drive him is obliquely suggested in the concluding lines of the poem. As Miss Nitchie has observed, the last sentence 'echoes the beginning and completes the circle of the poem'.[16] But it is significant that Wordsworth chose to recall two of the symbolic features of the Wye landscape: the oneness of its green hue and the ascending movement of the 'steep and lofty cliffs'.

'Dark Passages: Exploring "Tintern Abbey"', *Studies in Romanticism*, III, 1963, pp. 10–23.

[16] In *The Major English Romantic Poets*, ed. Clarence D. Thorpe, Carlos Baker, and Bennett Weaver (Carbondale, 1957), p. 15.

JOHN F. DANBY

Irony in *Simon Lee*

Wordsworth is a superb ironist in *Lyrical Ballads*. In the mixed mode
of the poems the poet can take up and lay down his masks. And with
each assumption or discard a new, sometimes excitingly dramatic, shift
of standpoint is possible. The narrator, the characters involved in the
story, the poet himself as the finally responsible assembler—these are
the three main levels at which the voices work. By changing the voice
one can step from one frame to another and back again. Stepping
apparently out of the frame of mere 'literature' altogether and into the
reader's own reality (his reality of experience and of judgement), con-
fronting the reader with the need to be aware of what he is judging with
as well as what he is judging—this is, above all, the Wordsworthian trick
in *Lyrical Ballads*. 'Simon Lee' is an outstanding example of it. No
wonder Wordsworth continued to stand by the poem as an example of
his art at its subtlest, its least pretentious and plainest.

'Simon Lee' ends with the following lines:

I've heard of hearts unkind, kind deeds
With coldness still returning.
Alas! the gratitude of men
Has oftener left me mourning.

'Simon Lee' exists as a poem, I think, to carry these lines to the reader
in the precise way it does: with the weight, the depth, the soberness, the
measured seriousness and overflowing tenderness that they have. It
exists, that is, to ensure the 'comprehensiveness in thinking and feeling'
which Wordsworth thought the great poet should possess and the good
reader acquire. How far Wordsworth has brought the reader in the poem
can be gauged by the difference between these last four lines and the
four lines with which the poem opens:

In the sweet shire of Cardigan,
Not far from pleasant Ivor-hall,
An old man dwells, a little man,
I've heard he once was tall.

As Wordsworth enters upon his task the pose he adopts is deceptive.
Until the last lines are reached the poem throughout plays with am-
biguities of tone. The reader is offered choices so various that he is
chary—if he is sufficiently aware—of plumping for any one of the
alternatives presented. Yet the various possibilities are pressed upon

us, so that the suspension of choice has to be willed. We are the more resolved not to commit ourselves precipitately because of the feeling that the poet is up to something, because he is himself highly sophisticated, and because, we suspect, what he ultimately intends is nothing at all so obvious or so slight as what seems to be going on.

The alternatives in these first four lines are fairly apparent. Because of '*sweet* shire'—with its conventional adjective—we might be with the mannered revivalism of Percy's *Reliques*. 'Pleasant' too could be the expected ballad word, and there is 'pleasaunce' (a far echo) to give local ballad colour to the otherwise unassuming counter. The word as applied to Ivor-hall guarantees the reliability of the anonymous Everyman who might be presumed to be speaking. He is well-disposed, even to the Squire, certainly to the traditional sanctities of the established countryside. But the poem is not allowed to settle here. The two lines that follow present a sharp alternative: the extremes of burlesque (it might be) or of unconsciously funny sadbrow earnestness. In any case, that is, we step outside the straightforward convention into something less familiar:

> An old man dwells, a little man,
> I've heard he once was tall.

The ludicrous, if we like, is brought teasingly near the surface. It is as though the reader were being challenged to recognize his first impulse to laugh, get over it at the outset, and dismiss it for the rest of the poem. (How we read the poem depends on how we deal with these temptations which Wordsworth puts in our path.) That we do struggle with our frivolousness or indelicacy is due, I think, to the sense that we are being deliberately tempted. Wordsworth, we feel, is watching our reaction, neither helping nor hindering us from keeping our balance, but he is aware, balanced and immensely assured himself. We are checked by the knowledge that this is the writing of a man both sophisticated and serious-minded. Then, when we look at the lines again, there is actually nothing to laugh at. The prose-sense that Wordsworth can always release to such sobering effect comes up in full force. All that the lines now say is that near pleasant Ivor-hall,

> An old man dwells, a little man,
> I've heard he once was tall.

If the speaker were clowning the second line would be said with bumpkin obliviousness to the paradoxical 'little man . . . once was tall'. We should then be with the Albert-saga of Stanley Holloway. The temptation so to read it seems thrust forward, but is so obvious that it is easily overcome. And there is enough in the poem already to suggest sobriety. The opening lines, in fact, with their 'little man . . . tall' contradiction present only a small puzzle, and the solution of the puzzle throws up something at once realistic and pathetic. Read naturally, too, their whole tenor is against cheapness either way. Though the ballads are in mind,

there are no mechanical ballad-metrics. There is a genuine and un-
affected music in them, but it is a naturally singing dialect voice we
hear—the regional voice of Wordsworth's Statesmen. Thus all four
lines could be read with something of solemnity, and possibly the con-
vinced Wordsworthian might prefer to take 'Simon Lee' throughout as
a uniformly sober performance. This would not, however, be strictly
conformable with the evidence. The tone of the poem is complicated
with ironies. We have to reject the temptation to be sentimental as well
as the temptation to laugh. The second half of the first stanza is deliberately intended to prevent a premature or misplaced seriousness.
We have nothing as yet to be serious about:

> Of years he has upon his back,
> No doubt, a burthen weighty;
> He says he is three score and ten,
> But others say he's eighty.

The more jaunty movement, the apparently casual 'no doubt' (though it
might mean, 'He certainly is *very* old, and no mistake!'), the 'He says—
others say' pit-pat, the flightiness and near-jocularity of the concluding
feminine rhyme (the sound of the word clashing ironically with the
sense)—all this makes over-earnestness impossible. Of set purpose
Wordsworth is interested in keeping the emotional temperature down,
and the reader in suspense.

The movement towards full seriousness of tone in this first part is
expertly managed. The delicacy of the shift is maybe better suggested
by a reading-aloud than by an analysis such as we are attempting. (The
danger in piecemeal exposition is that the passages isolated from their
context might collapse back on the burlesque or the banal or the solemn,
the very thing the subtle normalities and the freshness of the poem are
designed to avoid.) However, something of what Wordsworth is doing
can be focused on in his use of language. There is a significant repetition,
for example, of operative words and phrases, repetitions with new
increments of meaning. Thus, the sequence 'old–poor—poor–old' is
used twice. The first 'old' is in the lines already quoted concerning the
'old man'. The word 'poor' occurs in the verse following:

> A long blue livery-coat has he,
> That's fair behind, and fair before;
> Yet, meet him where you will, you see
> At once that he is poor.

The two words are combined in the next verses:

> His hunting feats have him bereft
> Of his right eye, as you may see;
> And then, what limbs those feats have left
> To poor old Simon Lee!

The sequence occurs a second time in the verses that move up to the climax of the first part:

> Old Ruth works out of doors with him,
> And does what Simon cannot do.
>
> A scrap of land they have, but they
> Are poorest of the poor.
>
> Few months of life has he in store,
> As he to you will tell,
> For still, the more he works, the more
> His poor old ancles swell.

The progress in each case is through the matter-of-fact senses of 'old' and 'poor' to the indulgently sympathetic. Age and poverty are first coolly seen as fact, and it is only then that the natural and appropriate concern for them is invited. A similar procedure is followed with the word 'little': first, 'a little man', the scientific sense predominating and then the frankly tender diminutive:

> And he is lean, and he is sick,
> His little body's all awry;
> His ancles they are swoln and thick:
> His legs are thin and dry.

One of the most telling repetitions is the second reference to Ivor-hall:

> His master's dead, and no one now
> Dwells in the hall of Ivor;
> Men, dogs, and horses, all are dead,
> He is the sole survivor.

The 'hall of Ivor' sounds grim and mockingly sardonic. The high-flownness of the phrase contrasts with the devastation and down-in-the-worldness the lines tell us about. The literariness, too, adds its point: it recalls violently the opposed associations of 'pleasant Ivor-hall', so that the levelling jacobinism of Time (the reality) echoes ironically against the toryism (the pretence) of the first and merely 'literary' form. In this third verse a new sombreness of tone and subject is reached:

> Men, dogs, and horses, all are dead

—the heavy monosyllables beat it out.

Wordsworth frames the personal tragedy of infirmity and poverty in the larger social tragedy of the decaying countryside. Throughout the first part, in fact, the dealings of Time with Man are concretely presented in social and personal terms together. The livery the old man wears reminds us of his former status as well as of his one-time vigour. Its out-of-placeness is two-fold, bringing home the pathos of the vanished security and the punyness of the form that can no longer fill it. Other details interchangeably suggest the private and the public worlds and the corrosion at work in each: the plot of ground enclosed 'from the heath', and Simon's being '*forced* to work, though weak'. By the end of this first part a whole era of social decay as well as personal decline has been suggested. At the end, such is Wordsworth's certainty that we are with him on his own terms, and are divested of our habitual notions concerning what is fit to be mentioned in poetry, that he risks his main, most confident, and most daring repetition—Simon's culminating infirmity, the scandalous particularity of the swollen ankles:

> Few months of life has he in store,
> As he to you will tell,
> For still, the more he works, the more
> His poor old ancles swell.

We are no longer listening to words as literature; we are listening to literature only as it can use words to present the significant facts. We want only the truth and 'comprehensiveness of thinking and feeling'.

Having forced the admission into poetry of such words and things as poor old ankles, Wordsworth turns (the moment is almost slily calculated) to apostrophize the reader:

> My gentle reader, I perceive
> How patiently you've waited,
> And I'm afraid that you expect
> Some tale will be related.
> O reader! had you in your mind
> Such stores as silent thought can bring,
> O gentle reader! you would find
> A tale in everything.
> What more I have to say is short,
> I hope you'll kindly take it;
> It is no tale, but should you think
> Perhaps a tale you'll make it.

The word 'gentle' is interestingly weighted. There is first the sense of 'submissive, amenable', and the condescension implied. There is also the opposite meaning, as in 'gentle and simple': 'well-born, polished and sophisticated, high in station'. The ambivalence reminds us of the reversible attitudes entertained to Ivor-hall, of the poet as ballad-retainer, and the poet as natural aristocrat. Underlying the two opposites and alternatives is the reconciling democratic meaning. To be gentle is to be tenderly considerate of others, willing to suffer them and suffer with them, to cherish and forbear—the feeling that equalizes inevitable inequalities and establishes the true fraternity. This is almost the basic meaning here. The reversibility of the superior-inferior relation makes possible a new kind of mutuality, an *equality* if we wish to use the word, but an equality that stands not on rightful demands so much as on reciprocal indulgences. This basic meaning of 'gentle' is supported by 'patiently' in the next line. To be patient is to submit, but the submission is from strength, as we might be patient in a storm, or with a child. In this instance the patience is ascribed to the Reader, not adopted by the Poet. Thus, in the twelve lines of the apostrophe, we are swung through the whole range of the not mutually exclusive attitudes involved, from that of indulgent patron to that of sturdy but deferential countryman:

> What more I have to say is short,
> I hope you'll kindly take it.

Wordsworth accurately catches the note of the peasant voice. He demonstrates too his command of 'the common word precise': here, the word 'kindly'—as belongs to man*kind*, with the *kind*ness we ought to have, and really do have at bottom: once we have reached bottom and discovered our *kind*.

This second movement unites writer and reader very intimately and yet leaves each remarkably independent. Within the relationship thus established a fuller 'comprehensiveness' is possible. The third part is now prepared for: the incident of the wood-cutting. Wordsworth tells the story with matter-of-fact faithfulness and even with a trace of humour. Simon's futility is pitiable but also laughable: naturally so to a young man who is himself firm and hearty and who knows he has age yet to come to:

> One summer day I chanced to see
> This old man doing all he could
> About the root of an old tree,
> A stump of rotten wood.
> The mattock totter'd in his hand;
> So vain was his endeavour
> That at the root of the old tree
> He might have worked for ever.

> 'You're overtasked, good Simon Lee,
> Give me your tool,' to him I said;
> And at the word right gladly he
> Receiv'd the proffer'd aid.
> I struck, and with a single blow
> The tangled root I sever'd,
> At which the poor old man so long
> And vainly had endeavour'd.

The ordinary tone is essential to the meaning. There is nothing extraordinary in Simon Lee's age and poverty. The impulse to lend him a hand is also perfectly natural. To call attention to it with undue emphasis would be to over-stress the common stuff of human nature that

is so easily, so promptly, and yet so casually being brought into play.
The great deepening of tone comes in the climax of the last verse:

> The tears into his eyes were brought,
> And thanks and praises seemed to run
> So fast out of his heart, I thought
> They never would have done.
> —I've heard of hearts unkind, kind deeds
> With coldness still returning.
> Alas! the gratitude of men
> Has oftener left me mourning.

'I've heard of hearts unkind'—we can hear the weariness, the impatience amounting to contempt, in Wordsworth's voice. He is conjuring up the whole sickening sphere of the moral and verbal cliché,
the set-pieces of life and literature, the jejune dogmas that encase the
mind, hardening it into impercipience or indifference. The literary
'winter wind' is never really *too* unkind—especially to the arrogant
self-righteousness it can so often subserve. The Jaques mentality, however, is as far from the Wordsworthian comprehensiveness as Arden is
from the enclosed bit of heath and mossed cottage of Simon Lee. Moral
emphases of a profound range and depth and normality are being re-
distributed as we read. The poet, as he later will say, has placed us 'in
the way of receiving from ordinary moral sensations another and more
salutary impression than we are accustomed to receive from them'.

The paradox of the final two lines is not a merely verbal trick, like the
Oscar Wilde inversion of commonplaces. And the reader is left to interpret its fullness as he best can. Through the course of the poem, but
culminating here, Wordsworth has effected his literary and psychic re-
education. The reader is restored to independence: independence of
the 'poetic', and independence (a more difficult thing) of the Poet—of
the writer, that is, as the provider of new 'attitudes to life', of novel
patterns and formulae of responses. He is restored to himself, to that
fresh air which he shares with the poet and with all men but which he
must breathe for himself. What, for example, we might be moved to
press on the poet, what is there in 'gratitude' to lead to 'mourning'? But
what in a case like this can the poet tell us that we don't know already,
and that his poem has not already put us in the way to realize? The
answer might include reference to the iniquities of society and the
harshness of Time in its dealings with men. Both these references
the poem makes. What mourning is it, though, that supervenes on the
young man's vigorous health and good spirits, and goes even deeper
than the tears that are brought to the eyes of a helpless old man? The
question is best left rhetorical. Answers here might themselves remain
mere rhetoric: such rhetoric as,

> The still, sad music of humanity

or even,

> Thoughts that do often lie too deep for tears.

The mourning becomes a Wordsworthian negative that seems immensely positive in its secure power, its capacity to feel the hurt and yet to embrace the hurtful.

From *The Simple Wordsworth*, London: Routledge and Kegan Paul, 1960, pp. 38–47.

EDWIN MORGAN

A Prelude to *The Prelude*

Wordsworth describes the main events of his life, as a child, at school, at Cambridge, in the Alps, in London, and in France, in considerable detail and with some reflection on them; the narrative is sometimes interrupted, but on the whole preserves its character as a personal history. Within this framework the central theme, as it emerges nakedly and purely from the events, is set forth with unmistakable clarity: the benign influence exerted by nature on the growing faculties of the whole man, the peculiar and perfect adaptation of nature to man, as of things made to interact, and the emergence of the complemental beauty of man's mind above but not severed from the beauty of nature. These aspects of the theme follow the course of the history. At the beginning, when the poet is a child, what is emphasized is the influence of natural forms in shaping his imagination and vision; at the end he has reached a point where the mind and character have developed a beauty in their own right, strengthened by human intercourse and sympathy but sustained still and always at the deeper wells of feeling in the presence of natural objects.

Such was the ultimate concern of the poet. Many events had to be related, however, and many sequences of thought followed out, for sincerity and completeness, which were certainly a part of his story but which tended to stultify his inspiration. These were usually scenes of human bustle and confusion, like the second-rate description of London streets in Book VII, and incursions into contemporary history and political and intellectual comment, as in Books IX–XI. For the first of these he was personally unsuited (as Lamb's letters amusingly remind us). His feelings were engaged by solitude and calm rather than by the hubbub of city crowds, and he was not able to write other than mechanically and dutifully about what he calls the 'perpetual whirl of trivial objects'. These things, not trivial in themselves, and indeed the centre of a huge mass of that very human life he was investigating, were trivial, disturbing, exasperating, and meaningless to Wordsworth; simplicity and the sense of order were wanting, and when they were absent he could not be at ease. Of the other less-than-successful part, dealing with 'residence in France', it is to be said that much of the material, reflections on theories and public events, was intractable, and behind the writing of the narrative part of these books we can often sense a deadening of impulse which seems to come from his knowledge that he is now to describe not advances and acquisitions but losses and retreats, the loss of his simple faith and a retreat from nature, and in such description he was cutting himself off from the two main sources of his strength. He had placed the books in a commanding position, and he gave the French matter very extended treatment, yet it appears in his life and can be used in the poem only as an incident which fortifies the deeper theme existing before it and victoriously returning after it. It had the great intellectual importance of being a testing-time for that strength Wordworth indicated himself as possessing, his lack (as he says) of 'trepidation for the end of things', but feelings so troubling to that strength were probably looked back on with positive distaste and certainly without the necessary fire of mind. The inadequacy of such determined, laboured, and even pompous writing as we often find in these books shows the main difficulty of the recollectional method. The imagination works only sympathetically; it is like the horse you take to the well but cannot force to drink; and when it is used to describe things past, its enthusiasm will not spring up unless what is being described has a lasting and present reality to the poet's feelings. The result for the reader is boredom, when the author, forgetting for a time that he must be communicatively lively even when recollectionally serious, buries himself in his photograph album and draws the dead leaves over his head. In prose, this boredom lurks in the most masterly and evocative reminiscential writers, such as Proust and Gide; we cannot be surprised to find it in the blank verse of a serious-minded poet. Wordsworth had felt and thought deeply about the French Revolution, but this had sunk down into his mind and had failed in the end to change the characteristics which existed before it began, though it gave them perhaps a profounder meaning; and it is those permanent characteristics, as I must now indicate, that Wordsworth had to learn how to tap and to use, if his verse was to be raised above the merely discursive level.

In the first book we find him exploring his theme in a variety of incidents, and indeed laying down the pattern he was later to elaborate again and again. There is simple description of the mere physical delight of activity in the open air, in the skating episode, where pure word-painting of scene and action in a self-contained form reaches high art; there is description of an episode simple in itself but illustrative of the sense of mystery in nature which was important to Wordsworth, in the night-piece where he speaks of snaring woodcocks in the hills and hearing the strange breathing and footsteps behind him; and there is the more detailed relation of an incident which is a powerful incentive to description but had also a greater significance as showing the early workings of conscience and terror, in the story of the stolen boat. This last example shows the beginnings of what is going to be Wordsworth's method: he has some point of his mental development to make clear, he wants to give it imaginative utterance, he looks back not along the line of his thoughts but into the actions he has been engaged in, he finds an incident where he himself in conjunction with nature in some form was visited or refreshed by the idea in question, and then the scene he has chosen is described from the viewpoint of its significance, and becomes alive in the act of writing because this interlocking of scene and thought is his permanent possession. It is the recollection of emotion, but the emotion is unabstractable from circumstance; it is the poetry of time and place, the 'faces and places, with the self which, as it could, loved them' of 'Little Gidding', In this first book Wordsworth gives us his own version of what has just been said, as if in a careless summing-up of his art: he is speaking of composition itself, of the memorial process, and he praises:

> those lovely forms
> And sweet sensations that throw back our life,
> And almost make remotest infancy
> A visible scene, on which the sun is shining.

With this should be compared some lines at the very end of the poem, where he says of the inception of his work:

> Anon I rose
> As if on wings, and saw beneath me stretched
> Vast prospect of the world which I had been
> And was; and hence this Song. . . .

Nothing could be clearer than this identification, in which his childhood, and then his entire life, are seen as sunlit vistas of physical landscape. The one beauty on which his imagination fed was the beauty of nature, and whatever else he knew to be beautiful, whatever he had to lay before his imagination for working up into poetry, had to be related to natural objects and seen by the light that shone on them. His subject was the growth of his mind, an abstract and intangible one for any poet, yet for Wordsworth there was scarcely a difficulty in that problem which was not solved, apart from the few 'dead' patches already referred to, since at the most important stages of his progress he unerringly directed his imagination towards concrete and living scenes, and in the blaze of feeling which enwrapped his recollection of these he was instantly warmed to an appreciation of his subject adequate for poetry. So it is that for all purposes the inward theme emerges clearly as the influence of nature on human feelings, because for Wordsworth all feelings of worth go back to the early promptings of nature, and even those sympathies which are awakened with a new interest in men themselves are found to have come originally from his first association with such men as work continually close to nature.

(In this connection one is reminded of a strangely and improbably similar forerunner. It is curious to observe how Lucretius, grappling with the intangibles of the *De Rerum Natura*, turns his great and passionate mind towards the same poetic solutions. 'The nature of things' becomes 'things in nature'; an automaton is given breath; the atoms and their laws grow visible in earth and sky and sea. Compare, for method, *De Rerum Natura*, Book V, 1183ff., where he describes men's primitive superstitious fear in the face of snow and hail, comets and constellations, thunder and lightning, and strengthened by these physical references bursts out with the lyrical and majestic

O genus infelix humanum . . . !

with *The Prelude*, Book XII, 225ff., where Wordsworth describes the 'visionary dreariness' of the moor, the gibbet, the pool, and the solitary woman walking into the wind, and the full feeling again works itself up to the surface suddenly in his cry

Oh! mystery of man . . . !

In both, there is a rare lyricism of the abstract, reached through the living forms of nature.)

In the presentation of Wordsworth's theme, the more important steps may be noted.

First comes his dedication to poetry in Book IV. The recounting of this great moment of his life, which it was evidently his duty to make an occasion of excellent verse, is initiated with a characteristic care. Just before it, he reminds the reader of his method by evolving an elaborate simile describing how his recollectional activity 'incumbent o'er the surface of past time' has been like that of a gazer from a boat into the depths of the water he passes through; it is a fine example of the suggestive power of a concrete description exactly denoting events which take place at a different level, in this case within the creating mind. Then comes the story of the midnight dance, the journey back through the fields at dawn, and the poet's sense of his destiny and meaning on this earth. What is most remarkable in this passage is that scarcely any words are required to state the theme of it in intellectual terms: it is a triumph of symbolic natural description. After we leave the clamour and gaiety of the dance behind and move on into the out-standingly evocative forms of the breaking day, and feel the joy of it, and the sense of refreshment and reawakening and preparation most aptly completed by the last picture of the labourers going out into the fields to begin their work, the reason for the whole description becomes so apparent that we know it is Wordsworth himself who seems just such a labourer meditating his work in such a dawn, and he needs only a few lines more to confirm for us the knowledge, in more abstract terms, of his dedication to the labour of verse.

My second example is from Book VI, at the point before the travellers enter the Simplon Pass. Here, the subject is the tremendous hunger of the imagination, unsatisfied except that it is itself a satisfaction to the soul, after that body of an invisible world which it surmises from the glimpses and flashes it has seen through the glory of natural objects:

> With hope it is, hope that can never die,
> Effort, and expectation, and desire,
> And something evermore about to be.

Again, the great passage is led up to and made immediate and actual by natural description. The traveller, eagerly setting out after a rest to conquer a new Alpine peak, has in fact taken the wrong path and must now descend; the Alps have been crossed, and there is no more climbing to be done; but his mind feeds on the imagined heights he must leave, and is loath to accept the fact that its longing cannot be satisfied, while at the same time recognizing that its desire is a sign of its greatness, that 'the passions of men . . . do immeasurably transcend their objects' (*The Convention of Cintra*). The whole incident, written in simple narrative style, yet becomes a symbol of considerable strength, because of this correspondence with the intellectual theme which is seen only after the reader has absorbed the influence of nature.

At a third point, in Book VIII, Wordsworth is concerned to relate some of the origins of his interest in his fellow-creatures and the grandeur he feels them to possess. As always, he works from the particular to the general, from one man to many; and from one occupation of man, and from one moment of that man's occupation when everything about it and him seemed to be significant. He describes a shepherd as seen by him at three different times: on the hills looming with his sheep through mist, walking in sudden sunset light, and at a great distance standing at the edge of the horizon. From these appearances, where a man moved into the poet's consciousness clothed with something of nature rather than human rags, even though it was only illusions of light, his imagination was stimulated at an early age to see men as creatures of dignity and power and beauty, which later became an appreciation of the mind:

> hence [he says] the human form
> To me became an index of delight,
> Of grace and honour, power and worthiness.

The mist, and the sunset light, and the distance, are in fact the mysteriousness, the radiance, and the remotely-fetched greatness present in Wordsworth's own imagination as he looks on man.

Fourthly, I take the account of the death of Robespierre in Book X, and the release of some of Wordsworth's anxiousness and wretchedness over the failure of the Revolution to be what it set out to be. As before, the mental liberation, here related in the scant words 'Robespierre is dead!', is almost imperceptibly won out of the physical; it needed only those words to round off the joy that was already filling his heart from another source. This source, the natural scene of the river estuary, the sun, and the clouded mountain-tops, has a peculiar aptness in the manner of its description. Any such atmosphere, glorious in itself, might have been depicted to show something of a general happiness, but Wordsworth makes it significant by suggesting in the occasion the very thought he is to reveal. This thought is the glad announcement, from a band of travellers on the beach, of the death of the French tyrant; and in the preceding description, where the peaks and clouds are met

> In consistory, like a diadem
> Or crown of burning seraphs as they sit
> In the empyrean,

we see as it were the grand type of such an announcement, as if the consistory in the clouds had come together as the fountain and authorization of the news, as if those seraphs were speaking to the imagination what the human travellers were next to speak to the intelligence. The echo of the Satanic consistory at the beginning of *Paradise Regained*, from which Wordsworth's usage very possibly arose, strengthens the sense of an assembly of spirits met to give forth some important utterance.

For a fifth example, there is the passage at the end of Book XII dealing with the death of Wordsworth's father. What the poet wants to emphasize is the power past incidents have over the mind when they recombine with present thoughts, rising up like admonitions, not changed in substance from what they were but given poignance by the passage of experience; and what in fact this emphasis amounts to, though nowhere stated, is an account of the combining power of past and present feelings in the making of poetry. The point he has to set out is that natural incidents, events taking place fully in the outdoor world of nature or closely associated with that world, are impressed on the memory according to the human feeling of joy or fear or mystery surrounding them, and what seems at the time to be a power these scenes themselves possess is afterwards known to have been a reflection of the mind contemplating them by its 'auxiliar light'. Again he makes everything grow out of the concrete setting, and this time there are two stages of emergence from it. First he describes, in simple narrative with no comment, the desolate wild misty day on the crag where he is waiting impatiently for a sight of the horses that are to take him home. Then he tells how, after his father's death, that scene returned vividly to his mind, with all its imagery become symbols of bleakness, of loneliness, and of a more than physical cold. Lastly he recalls more recent visitations of that imagery, mingling suddenly with his ordinary thoughts for no reason apparent to the intelligence, but effecting in them a grave displacement and disturbance, various according as the emotion in which they first arose is agreeable or harsh to his present feeling. From these hints the reader must take what he can. Wordsworth is probing, in an almost Lucretian fashion, some of the seminal 'hiding-places of man's power':

> sic alid ex alio per te tute ipse videre
> talibus in rebus poteris caecasque latebras
> insinuare omnis et verum protrahere inde.
>
> (I. 407–9)

A sixth and final point is taken from the last book, from the incident of the night on Snowdon. As this is the last great example of the process, so it is also the best; in it Wordsworth now fully explores the potentialities of his chosen method. In the most awesome of all his pictures he builds up the vast prospect of mountain-tops, clouds, moon, and stars, seen like another sea stretching out from Snowdon into the Atlantic main, while from below he hears the roaring of torrents mounting up into the calm. Then with neither hedging nor pause, but rather with a full consciousness of adequacy, he plunges into the correspondence, one of the most audacious images in our poetry and perhaps the surest measure of his own mind. The mountain, with all the forms of clouds and waters surrounding and washing it, in his symbol of 'a majestic intellect' raised far above (but still a part of) the plain of ordinary feeling; the clouds and mists which stream out from its summit into the unbounded spaces above the Atlantic are the thoughts sent out by imagination over the bottomless depths of knowledge; and the sound of the torrents underneath is heard as the glad thoughts or poems of the thinker or imaginer issue from the profound unseen wells and springs of his nature. Just as the mountain appeared to lean up and out into space, so it becomes

> the emblem of a mind
> That feeds upon infinity.

And as the image here was particularly large and grand, so the verse which follows it is ample and sustained; and we have in fact not simply the majesty of the mountain, and from that the imagined majesty of the intellect, but finally an example of such majesty as that intellect in action can create. Thus we are first made to feel the power of the circumstantial situation; then we are introduced to the analogy describing the symbol; and in the end we have an application in poetry of the body of what has been said.

In all these examples we can watch Wordsworth coming gradually to a realization of where and how his theme and his power were to be fused. He had to find out, from many kinds of description, from discursive reasoning, and from the analogies of tales and incidents, that anything he was to recreate through recollection must spring from the ground of the natural world, whether in itself a human emotion, an intellectual idea, or an article of faith; and he had to learn, up to the concluding book of *The Prelude*, how to infuse into his natural descriptions that absolute suggestive correspondence which makes them reveal and underscore the theme itself. He had to overcome the abstractness of his subject not by writing of abstractions in thick concrete imagery, as Shakespeare did, but by giving clear brilliant pictures separated from the intellectual content while imaginatively evoking it as something about to be told, this being necessitated by the recollectional method contemplating actual incidents in singleness.

The resulting work, although it is a poem, is a poem of a very peculiar kind. It is rightly named 'The Prelude', because it is the prelude to an unwritten poem; but in the business of preparing for that poem it has drained off so much life from the imaginary work still gestating in Wordsworth's mind that we have another case of the child being father of the man—even a child unborn. *The Prelude* is not, therefore, completely unified in either intention or method. It is a record of the past; a creation of poetry out of the interaction of past and present; and a trial flight for imagined poetry of the future. Wordsworth's great victory came from his realization that these three processes had to find, and could find, a common meeting-ground.

From 'A Prelude to *The Prelude*', *Essays in Criticism*, V, 1955, pp. 341–53 (344–53).

Imagination in *The Prelude*, I and VI

The Prelude opens with a success immediately followed by a failure. Released from the 'vast city' and anticipating a new freedom, the poet pours out a rush of fifty lines: 'poetic numbers came / Spontaneously to clothe in priestly robe / A renovated spirit' (I. 51–3).[1] Here is the consecration, the promise of poetry as a sacrament, a gift efficacious beyond the moment. Why should a chance inspiration assume such significance? The reason is that Wordsworth was not used to make 'A present joy the matter of a song'; yet here, apparently, is evidence that he may soon become self-creative, or need no more than a 'gentle breeze' (the untraditional muse of the epic's opening) to produce a tempest of poetry. 'Matins and vespers of harmonious verse!' is the hope held out to him, and having punctually performed matins the poet is content to slacken, to be gradually calmed by the clear autumn afternoon.

He meditates beneath a tree on a great poetic work soon to be begun. The sun sets, and city smoke is 'ruralized' by distance. He starts to continue his journey, but now it is clearly time for vespers:

It was a splendid evening, and my soul
Once more made trial of her strength, nor lacked
Aeolian visitations. (I. 94–6)

An outside splendour challenges the creative mind. Is the poet strong enough to answer it spontaneously, as if he needed only a suggestion, the first chord?

but the harp
Was soon defrauded, and the banded host
Of harmony dispersed in straggling sounds,
And lastly utter silence! 'Be it so;
Why think of any thing but present good?' (I. 96–100)

Wordsworth once again sees present good, like present joy, strangely opposed to the quickening of verse. The poetic outburst which he had

[1] Throughout this book, quotations from *The Prelude* (unless otherwise stated) are from the 1850 text as printed by De Selincourt and Darbishire in *William Wordsworth, The Prelude* (Oxford, 1959), short-titled *Prelude*. Charles Moorman has established that there is a pattern to the opening episode, although I will differ from him in my view of the pattern and its meaning. See 'Wordsworth's *Prelude: I, 1–269,*' *MLN*, 72 (1957), 416–20. R. D. Havens, *The Mind of a Poet* (Baltimore, 1941), pp. 290 ff., had failed to see any pattern.

considered a religious thing ('punctual service high . . . holy services') is now disdained as profane and *servile*:

> So, like a home-bound labourer I pursued
> My way beneath the mellowing sun, that shed
> Mild influence; nor left in me one wish
> Again to bend the Sabbath of that time
> To a servile yoke. (I. 101–5)

His reversal of mood is surprisingly complete. One who, at the impassioned outset of his reflections, had been so sure of the freely creative, autonomous nature of his poetic soul that famous passages on the emancipated spirit—from *Paradise Lost* and Exodus[2]—swell the current of his verse, while he thinks to possess total freedom of choice,

> now free,
> Free as a bird to settle where I will (I. 8–9)

that same person now writes of himself, with a slight echo of Gray's *Elegy*:

> So, like a home-bound labourer I pursued
> My way.

The meaning of the reversal is not immediately clear. It does not deject the poet; it endows him, on the contrary, with a Chaucerian kind of cheer and leisure:

> What need of many words;
> A pleasant loitering journey, through three days
> Continued, brought me to my hermitage.
> I spare to tell of what ensued, the life
> In common things—the endless store of things. (I. 105–9)

The form of the reversal is that of a return to nature, at least to its rhythm. For the moment no haste remains, no tempest, no impatience of spirit. It is the mood of the hawthorn shade, of a portion of Wordsworth's Cambridge days, when he laughed with Chaucer and heard him, while birds sang, tell tales of love (III. 278–81).

In the exultant first lines of *The Prelude*, Wordsworth had foreseen the spirit's power to become self-creative. Though fostered by nature it eventually outgrows its dependence, sings and storms at will (I. 33–38). The poet's anticipation of autonomy is probably less a matter of pride than of necessity: he will steal the initiative from nature so as to freely serve or sustain the natural world should its hold on the affections slacken. His poetic power, though admittedly in nature's gift, must perpetuate, like consecration, vital if transitory feelings. Without poetry the supreme moment is nothing.

---

[2] Emancipated—but through exile. For the allusions to *Paradise Lost* and Exodus, see *Prelude* I, 14 and 16–18.

Dear Liberty! Yet what would it avail
But for a gift that consecrates the joy? (I. 31–2)

But he is taught that the desire for immediate consecrations is a wrong form of worship. The world demands a devotion less external and wilful, a wise passiveness which the creative will may profane. The tempest 'vexing its own creation' is replaced by a 'mellowing sun, that shed/ Mild influence'. Nature keeps the initiative. The mind at its most free is still part of a deep mood of weathers.

Wordsworth's failure to consecrate, through verse, the splendid evening is only the last event in this reversal. It begins with the poet placing (so to say) the cart before the horse, Poetry before Nature: 'To the open fields I told / A prophecy: poetic numbers came...' (I. 50 ff.). He never, of course, forgets the double agency of inward and outward which informs every act of poetry. So his heart's frost is said to be broken by both outer and inner winds (I. 38 ff.)[3] Such reciprocity is at the heart of all his poems. Yet he continually anticipates a movement of transcendence: Nature proposes but the Poet disposes. Just as the breeze engendered in the mind a self-quickening tempest, so poetry, the voice from that tempest, re-echoing in the mind whence it came, seems to increase there its perfection (I. 55 ff.). The origin of the whole moves farther from its starting point in the external world. A *personal* agent replaces that of nature: 'I paced on ... down I sate ... slackening my thoughts by choice' (I. 60 ff.). There is a world of difference between this subtle bravado and the ascendancy of *impersonal* constructions in the final episode: 'Be it so; / Why think of any thing but ... What need of many words? ... I pursued/My way ... A pleasant loitering journey ... brought me to my hermitage'.

This change, admittedly, is almost too fine for common language. Syntax becomes a major device but not a consistent one. In the 1850 text, while the poet muses in the green, shady place, certain neoclassical patterns, such as the noble passive combined with synecdoche, create an atmosphere in which personal and impersonal, active and passive, blend strongly:

Many were the thoughts
Encouraged and dismissed, till choice was made
Of a known Vale, whither my feet should turn. (I. 70–2)

Devices still more subtle come into play. In the passage immediately preceding, Wordsworth describes the quiet autumn afternoon:

a day
With silver clouds, and sunshine on the grass,
And in the sheltered and the sheltering grove
A perfect stillness. (I. 67–70)

[3] Cf. M. H. Abrams, 'The Correspondent Breeze: A Romantic Metaphor', in *English Romantic Poets*, ed. Abrams (Galaxy paperback, New York, 1960), pp. 37–54.

'Sheltered and sheltering'—typical Wordsworthian verbosity? The redundance, however, does suggest that whatever is happening here happens in more than one place; compare 'silver clouds, and sunshine on the grass'. The locus doubles, redoubles: that two-fold agency which seems to centre on the poet is active all around to the same incremental effect. The grove, sheltered, shelters in turn, and makes 'A perfect stillness'. The poet, in a sense, is only a single focus to something universally active. He muses on this intensifying stillness, and within him rises a picture, gazing on which with *growing* love 'a higher power/ Than Fancy' enters to affirm his musings. The reciprocal and incremental movement, mentioned explicitly in I. 31 ff., occurs this time quite unself-consciously, clearly within the setting and through the general influences of Nature.

No wonder, then, that the city, which the poet still strove to shake off in the first lines, appears now not only distant but also 'ruralized', taking on the colours of nature, as enclosed by it as the poet's own thought. The last act of the reversal is the episode of the splendid sunset. Wordsworth not only cannot, he *need* not steal the initiative from nature. Her locus is universal, not individual; she acts by expedients deeper than will or thought. Wordsworth's failure intensifies his sense of a principle of generosity in nature. That initial cry of faith, 'I cannot miss my way' (I. 18), becomes true, but not because of his own power. The song loses its way.

Wordsworth's first experience is symptomatic of his creative difficulties. One impulse vexes the creative spirit into self-dependence, the other exhibits nature as that spirit's highest object. The poet is driven at the same time from and toward the external world. No sooner has he begun to enjoy his Chaucerian leisure than restiveness breaks in. The 'pilgrim', despite 'the life/In common things—the endless store of things', cannot rest content with his hermitage's sabbath. Higher hopes, 'airy phantasies', clamour for life (I. 114 ff.). The poet's account of his creative difficulties (I. 146–269) documents in full his vacillation between a natural and a more than natural theme, between a Romantic tale and one of 'natural heroes', or 'a tale from my own heart' and 'some philosophic song'—but he adds, swinging back to the more humble, 'Of Truth that cherishes our daily life'. Is this indeterminacy the end at which nature aims, this curious and never fully clarified restlessness the ultimate confession of his poetry?

It would be hard, in that case, to think of *The Prelude* as describing the 'growth of a poet's mind'; for what the first part of Book I records is, primarily, Wordsworth's failure to be a visionary or epic poet in the tradition of Spenser and Milton. No poem of epic length or ambition ever started like his. The epic poet begins confidently by stating his subject, boasts a little about the valour of his attempt, and calls on the Muse to help him. Yet Wordsworth's confident opening is deceptive. He starts indeed with a rush of verses which are in fact a kind of self-quotation, because his subject is poetry or the mind which has separated

from nature and here celebrates its coming-of-age by generously
returning to it. After this one moment of confidence, all is problematic.
The song loses its way, the proud opening is followed by an experience
of aphasia, and Wordsworth begins the story of the growth of his mind
to prove, at least to himself, that nature had intended him to be a poet.
Was it for this, he asks, for this timidity or indecision, that nature spent
all her care (I. 269 ff.)? Did not nature, by a process of both accom-
modation and weaning, foster the spirit's autonomy from childhood on?
Yet when the spirit tries to seize the initiative, to quicken of itself like
Ezekiel's chariot, either nature humbles it or Wordsworth humbles himself before her. 'Thus my days', says Wordsworth sadly, 'are past/In
contradiction; with no skill to part/Vague longing, haply bred by want
of power,/From paramount impulse not to be withstood,/A timorous
capacity from prudence, / From circumspection, infinite delay'
(I. 237–42).

Wordsworth never achieved his philosophic song. Prelude and 'Excursion' are no more than 'ante-chapels' to the 'gothic church' of his
unfinished work. An unresolved opposition between Imagination and
Nature prevents him from becoming a visionary poet. It is a paradox,
though not an unfruitful one, that he should scrupulously record
nature's workmanship, which prepares the soul for its independence
from sense-experience, yet refrain to use that independence out of
respect of nature. His greatest verse *still takes its origin* in the memory of
given experiences to which he is often pedantically faithful. He adheres,
apparently against nature, to natural fact.

There are many who feel that Wordsworth could have been as great
a poet as Milton but for this return to nature, this shrinking from
visionary subjects. Is Wordsworth afraid of his own imagination? Now
we have, in The Prelude, an exceptional incident in which the poet
comes, as it were, face to face with his imagination. This incident has
many points in common with the opening event of The Prelude; it also,
for example, tells the story of a failure of the mind vis-à-vis the external
world. I refer to the poet's crossing of the Alps, in which his adven-
turous spirit is again rebuffed by nature, though by its strong absence
rather than presence. His mind, desperately and unself-knowingly in
search of a nature adequate to deep childhood impressions, finds
instead *itself*, and has to acknowledge that nature is no longer its proper
subject or home. Despite this recognition, Wordsworth continues to
bend back the energy of his mind and of his poem to nature, but not
before we have learned the secret behind his fidelity.

Having finished his third year of studies at Cambridge, Wordsworth
goes on a walking tour of France and Switzerland. It is the summer of
1790, the French Revolution has achieved its greatest success and acts
as a subtle, though, in the following books, increasingly human background to his concern with nature. Setting out to cross the Alps by way
of the Simplon Pass, he and a friend are separated from their com-
panions and try to ascend by themselves. After climbing some time and

not overtaking anyone, they meet a peasant who tells them they must return to their starting point and follow a stream down instead of further ascending, i.e. they had already, and without knowing it, crossed the Alps. Disappointed, 'For still we had hopes that pointed to the clouds', they start downward beset by a 'melancholy slackening', which, however, is soon dislodged (VI. 557-91, 616 ff.).

This naive event stands, however, within a larger, interdependent series of happenings: an unexpected revelation comes almost immediately (624-40), and the sequence is preceded by a parallel disappointment with the natural world followed by a compensatory vision (523 ff.). In addition to this pattern of blankness and revelation, of the soulless image and the sudden renewed immediacy of nature, we find a strange instance of the past flowing into the present. Wordsworth, after telling the story of his disappointment, is suddenly, in the very moment of composition, overpowered by a feeling of glory to which he gives expression in rapturous, almost self-obscuring lines (VI. 592 ff.). Not until the moment of composition, some fourteen years after the event,[4] does the real reason behind his upward climb and subsequent melancholy slackening strike home; and it strikes so hard that he gives to the power in him, revealed by the extinction of the immediate external motive (his desire to cross the Alps) and by the abyss of intervening years, the explicit name Imagination:

> Imagination—here the Power so called
> Through sad incompetence of human speech,
> That awful Power rose from the mind's abyss
> Like an unfathered vapour that enwraps,
> At once, some lonely traveller. I was lost;
> Halted without an effort to break through;
> But to my conscious soul I now can say—
> 'I recognize thy glory.' (VI. 592-99)

Thus Wordsworth's failure vis-à-vis nature (or its failure vis-à-vis him) is doubly redeemed. After descending, and passing through a gloomy strait (621 ff.), he encounters a magnificent view. And crossing, one might say, the gloomy gulf of time, his disappointment becomes retrospectively a prophetic instance of that blindness to the external world which is the tragic, pervasive, and necessary condition of the mature poet. His failure of 1790 taught him gently what now (1804) literally *blinds* him: the independence of imagination from nature.

I cannot miss my way, the poet exults in the opening verses of *The Prelude*. And he cannot, as long as he respects the guidance of nature, which leads him along a gradual via negativa to make his soul more than 'a mere pensioner/On outward forms' (VI. 737 f.). It is not easy, however, to 'follow Nature'. The path, in fact, becomes so circuitous that a

---

[4] That the rising up of imagination occurred as Wordsworth was remembering his disappointment rather than immediately after it (i.e. in 1804, not in 1790) was first pointed out by W. G. Fraser in *TLS* (April 4, 1929), p. 276.

poet follows least when he thinks he follows most. For he must cross a strait where the external image is lost yet suddenly revived with more than original immediacy. Thus a gentle breeze, in the first book, calls forth a tempest of verse, but a splendid evening wanes into silence. A magnificent hope, in the sixth book, dies for lack of sensuous food, but fourteen years later the simple memory of failure calls up that hope in a magnificent tempest of verse. When the external stimulus is too clearly present the poet falls mute and corroborates Blake's strongest objection: 'Natural Objects always did and now do weaken, deaden, and obliterate Imagination in Me'.[5] The poet is forced to discover the autonomy of his imagination, its independence from present joy, from strong outward stimuli—but this discovery, which means a passing of the initiative from nature to imagination, is brought on gradually, mercifully.

Wordsworth does not sustain the encounter with Imagination. His direct cry is broken off, replaced by an impersonal construction—'here the Power'. It is not Imagination but his 'conscious soul' he addresses directly in the lines that follow. What, in any case, is the soul to do with its extreme recognition? It has glimpsed the height of its freedom. At the end of his apostrophe to Imagination, Wordsworth repeats the idea that the soul is halted by its discovery, as a traveller by a sudden bank of mist. But the simile this time suggests not only a divorce from but also (proleptically) a return to nature on the part of the soul,

> Strong in herself and in beatitude
> That hides her, like the mighty flood of Nile
> Poured from his fount of Abyssinian clouds
> To fertilise the whole Egyptian plain. (VI. 613–16)

From *Wordsworth's Poetry: 1787–1814*, New Haven and London: Yale University Press, 1964, pp. 33–42.

[5] Marginalia to Volume I of Wordsworth's *Poems* of 1815. I may venture the opinion that Wordsworth, at the beginning of *The Prelude*, goes back to nature not to increase his chances of sensation but rather to emancipate his mind from immediate external excitements, the 'gross and violent stimulants' (1800 Preface to *Lyrical Ballads*) of the city he leaves behind him.

ALEC KING

The Two Childhoods in the
Immortality Ode

One of the keys to an understanding of Wordsworth's feeling for childhood as a state of grace, and its relation to the mature vision of man, is the 'Immortality Ode'.

The heart of the poem is a double vision of childhood, the childhood that we see being busily lived through by children and which we ourselves lived through, and the childhood which we carry within us like a memory, and which while grounded in our earliest years stays with us into adult life for good or evil.

These two childhoods may be called, for convenience, visible childhood and invisible childhood. We are mostly aware of the visible childhood in children. It is the mother, as Yeats understood, who knows best the invisible childhood, who in her 'passion, piety, or affection' knows the 'shape upon her lap' as a 'Presence' that symbolizes 'all heavenly glory' and that mocks 'man's enterprise'.[1]

Wordsworth distinguishes these two childhoods, not only by what he says of each, but by different languages. The visible childhood of the 'six year darling of a pigmy size' is lived openly and busily for us in the factual language of the VIIth stanza, in the imitative play of the little actor. The invisible childhood is referred to, as it must be, in terms of metaphor and myth, especially in the VIIIth stanza, with its names for a child like 'thou best philosopher', 'thou eye among the blind'.

It is for the sake of grasping the mysterious nature of invisible childhood that Wordsworth 'invented' the myth of pre-existence. The note he dictated to Miss Fenwick is clear on this. He disclaims any intention of preaching a belief in a prior state of existence. 'It is far too shadowy a notion to be recommended to faith', Wordsworth says, 'but it has', he suggests, 'entered into the popular creeds of many nations', and 'when I was impelled to write this Poem I took hold of the notion of pre-existence as having sufficient foundation in humanity for authorizing me to make for my purpose the best use of it I could as a Poet.'[2] The soul enters human life at our birth as an episode in its immortal life. It is exiled for a time from its divine home, but in its first years it does not forget its home or the divine light which is its source. Only gradually does the world narrow down into a prison, the vision cloud, the light

---

[1] 'Among School Children' (*Collected Poems*, London, 1958, p. 242).
[2] *Works*, IV, p. 464.

fail. This flat account of stanza V suggests only the bare structure of the image, its narrative form. The beauty and effectiveness of the image are due to our seeing the process not from the outside, but from the inside; and it is this which makes us aware of the pathos of the relation of our lives to our own immortality. The light of the soul that we inherit transfigures all we see. 'Heaven lies *about* us in our infancy', not transcendentally remote. Our first world is 'actual, divine and true'. The joy of childhood is a 'strain of the Earth's sweet being in the beginning, in Eden garden'. Only the compelling need to grow into human maturity narrows and shadows this divine largeness. We grow into the prison of our days, as we grow up; and the fresh transfiguring light of the dawn of human life revealing all things to our awakened senses is gradually changed *by us* into a common light that illuminates mere objects.

Imaginatively read, as Wordsworth invites us to read it, this stanza is not in the least like a statement of belief in pre-existence. It is the account of our universal human experience, in terms of myth. And it relates itself, as it must, to the whole meaning of incarnation:

That glorious Form, that Light unsufferable . . .
He laid aside; and here with us to be,
Forsook the Courts of everlasting Day,
And chose with us a darksom House of mortal Clay.[3]

Man does not choose his darksom House, he is born into it. In this stanza Wordsworth is presenting to us the dilemma of all human incarnation, that the gift of life is perplexed by the living form and materials of its incarnation. The very 'juice and joy' of that springtime innocence and purity which is our birthright, is itself the energy which compels us away from the heaven of invisible childhood. The youth *must* travel. And this is why, as Wordsworth makes us see in the next stanza, Earth as our mother must make the soul, the life given to us, feel at home here, not because the absolute glory of life and its imperial source is something she does not acknowledge or desire, but because her foster-child must know imperial life as she knows it, embodied in the material substance of the natural world. There is, though, in the stanza, a peculiarly Wordsworthian tenderness towards nature, as if he needed to express what perhaps all creative artists feel in their dealings with the material substance of their art—a delight in being bodily at home, comforted by the enclasping world and its solidity, unexposed to too much nakedness of glory.

In these two stanzas Wordsworth has in effect incarnated the soul of life in its earthly dress. He has brought together the invisible and the visible childhood of man as they must exist together. In the next stanza he turns wholly to the visible child, in a language of affectionate and ironic realism. The child must travel into the business of human activity, practising like a little actor his coming roles, imitating what he sees. But

---

[3] Milton's 'On the Morning of Christ's Nativity', Proem, Verse II.

immediately, in the next stanza, Wordsworth recalls the mystery of this new life which seeks sophistication with such absorbed attention, and yet which carries within it an invisible blessedness, a way of Being, apparently unregarded and unprized, which is 'the fountain light of all our day' and the 'master light of all our seeing'. The truth of this unconsoling paradox is created for us in the language, necessarily, of myth and metaphor, and with astonishing imaginative sureness, especially in the way we are held, in the poetry, both within the life of the child and above it, remembering from our height of adult maturity the invisible childhood which we were blessed with and which we did not want. The names for the Child—Philosopher, Prophet, Seer—are deliberately an outrage on our understanding, when we recall the visible child and his efforts to surmount his pygmy size, his weakness of power and skill, his longing for and his inevitable discovery of what, when we all find it, is a yoke. But the names, by their very unchildlikeness of tone, point at the meaning of what was given with the gift of life to a new creature, of what 'we are toiling all our lives to find', of what we are trying always to remember; the immensity of grace, absoluteness of being, whose strength and freedom we only understand when we have lost the first positive innocence which is its proper channel.

No human being can ever quite deal with this dilemma in experience; for a young creature must find the weakness of his visible childhood intolerable in his efforts to be grown up; and the strength of his invisible childhood (the immortality of Life in him) is inevitably confused and corrupted by his efforts, by the 'weight of custom, heavy as frost', by all the patterned responses and the learned gestures through which his ego is confirmed. Yet the final wisdom of life has always been recognized as grounded in the virtues of the 'child' as symbol, in the unself-regarding obedience to the life of things, the unanxious defenceless giving away of himself, the naked exposure of nerve, the candid regard of innocence which is so disarming because it is imaginative identity purified of all designing egotism, the general love of life which is so strong and active that it is best seen as a divine appetite. The 'child's' vision is uncorrupted by explanatory language; he is a pure instance of the one life both within and without before the self-conscious need to make a place for himself by talk and action has arisen; he is as yet unloosed from the universal life, as yet unmindful of his separate existence which will have to be so laboriously constructed, and which will be the 'dark glass' through which he begins to see all things, no longer 'face to face'; he is the 'Eye among the blind', that 'deaf and silent read'st the eternal deep haunted for ever by the eternal mind'.

How to hold the 'child' within oneself, to remember it as an always potentially present state of being, as our own real immortality—to hold this within ourselves even while we are hauling and pushing our visible childhood with the help and the examples of our elders into the prescribed patterns of adult life?—this is what the poem asks and asks. It cannot be answered in precept. The weakness and dependence of the

'child' is his strength, since it is part of his willingness to be cared for by
whatever fulfils him with life; and it is this weakness and dependence
which we try to struggle out of as quickly as possible, since we wish to
stand on our own feet. We cannot avoid the earnest pains with which we
provoke the years to bring the inevitable yoke; and it was Wordsworth's deep wisdom that he saw how we must remember our invisible
childhood as we grow older, since we cannot preserve it; and that the
mystery of childhood is that we do not know the blessedness we were
born into until we remember it after it has been lost, and in remembering it we remake our inner lives, we re-create ourselves through imagination and memory; knowing invisible childhood, in fact, not in itself, but
as a glimpse of divine maturity. The childlike maturity of the 'Saint' has
always criticized both our childishness and our attempts to supplant it
by sophistication.

It is this which the final stanza of the poem keeps in our minds. When
we have been matured by living, we may, if we are wise, not look away
from the immortality of our own life, nor look back at it through the
mists of the years in longing, but look inward to find it again, and to love
it even more than when we belonged to it in unconscious childhood.
For the presence and meaning of our invisible childhood is for our
anxious egotism something peculiarly precious and even miraculous; a
kind of rebirth, although momentary, in which the ordinarily unnoticed
things may become the channel through which we feel the depth and
splendour of the life we belong to.

The whole of stanzas IX and X is leading us to this final point.
Wordsworth follows the uncertainty of this process in stanza IX. Our
invisible childhood is 'fugitive', it dies away, but remains a perpetual
possibility, as light which has gone out in a fire still stays to be reborn
from the embers. Light is not born from embers by its own will but by a
breath from outside: it is not we but nature that remembers what *was*
so fugitive. Here is Wordsworth's faith in the nature which he has called
a homely nurse, which he trusts to keep alive in us our immortal childhood by her own way of showing us in her material images symbols of
the 'light that never was on sea or land'. Wordsworth is completely
honest and true to his own imagination, in the way he sees this operation
of nature. Our visible childhood is delight and liberty, activity, hope;
the transfiguring of objects in the light of the mind which nature en-
courages in us is felt by the visible child with misgiving and bewilderment. The falling and vanishing into 'thought' of the solid world, the
child's sense that what he is looking at is becoming insubstantial, a part
of his own mind, so that like the child Wordsworth himself he grasps
at a wall or tree to recall himself to the solid earth—this may arouse a
kind of fear,[4] although it is in fact part of the strength of the invisible
child, the 'seer blest'. It will become, in the artist, the very process
of his vision.

[4] See the note to Miss Fenwick, *Works*, IV, p. 463.

It is very moving to see how, in drawing and painting, children genuinely solve this problem of longing to grasp at a substantial world and yet to paint their dream-like apprehension of it. The characteristic painting of a child is full of shapes that have the solid angularity, the abruptness of actual objects; one bumps into them; they are the excited discovery of the life of objects. And yet the whole painting is dominated by inward vision, shadowy recollections and feelings, which inform the whole work with a naive power. Children paint like true artists; they create or invent lumps of matter to fill space, and the inventive process is dominated by inward vision which at the same time makes every blot and line a living gesture. This truthful origin of their art often makes the vague imitativeness of competent but second-rate mature artists look boring. But children's paintings are not great art, not chiefly because children are technically naive, but because they are caught in the paradox that Wordsworth defines for us in the Ode. The mature artist will lose inevitably the 'freshness of a dream' which so frequently startles us in a child's painting; but if he has known the 'primal sympathy which, having been, must ever be', he comes to 'love the brooks . . . even more than when he tripped lightly as they'; and can find in the meanest objects 'thoughts that do often lie too deep for tears'. The child paints his world and himself with fresh but shallow gestures; there does not rise in him, to guide his vision, the full power of his immortal invisible human childhood, for he is turning away from it. He is not only turning away from it, he has (so to speak) never learnt to exercise it in the face of that intractable experience which maturity brings. Only the mature artist, no longer child in fact, knows and invites this innocent visionary power in its fulness, for he turns towards it out of the fragmentation of common existence as a special power to 'see into the life of things'. Wordsworth could not help knowing, as an artist, that, though in all this the child is father to the man and bequeaths his primal wealth to the man, yet it is the mature man who knows what wealth it is, and how it may be used as the 'master light of all his seeing'. Nothing is more startling in the painting of a great master (leaving aside all relish of a sophisticated technique) than the way it holds within itself the paradox of this poem; the candour and directness of its childlike vision and the immense mature richness of what it is 'looking at'. The great artist is an 'eye among the blind', a 'seer blest', one 'haunted by the eternal mind'; and he knows (or is it 'remembers'?) that this visionary power is released as a gift only if he is unselfconsciously preoccupied with a practical task, daubing, chiselling, moving words around into tunable order, so that his 'soul's immensity' can find its proper language uncorrupted by most unchildlike murmurs of self-congratulation. In all this the artist takes to himself his invisible childhood. But unlike the real child, he welcomes the 'obstinate questionings', the 'fallings' and 'vanishings', as he moves about 'in worlds not realised', for it is through these that he is impelled to discover the images that have 'power to make our noisy years seem moments in the being of the eternal Silence'.

And, above all unlike that of a real child, his vision is deepened and tensioned by mature experience of what requires, in all of us, the transfiguring power.

The great work of art feels dense with a potentially refractory life that has been brought miraculously to composure, and its order and beauty are therefore intensely exciting. By comparison the child's vision in his painting is praeternaturally limpid, even if his images are horrific as they sometimes are; for he inhabits a world unconscious of anything but the effortless flow of living things and his imaginative identity with them. The ambiguity of Eden is always a perplexity; for the children who really live there do not know they want it and are always trying to leave; and the adults who dream of its effortless joys do so from human fatigue and confusion. How right Milton was not to give us first the picture of an earthly paradise; but to start by building up in our minds the worlds of hell and heaven, the tension of evil and good, which gives Paradise all its meaning as a state in which all the vital energies of the world, potential for good and evil, are concordant, obedient to their centre. Adam and Eve, in their unfallen state, would have painted pictures like children. Only after their expulsion from Eden would they have been able to create great works, knowing then the terrible liveliness of God which they had lost and were trying to find again.

Wordsworth's poem is, of course, also a Paradise Lost; and it starts, unlike Milton's work, with man bereft, bewildered by his loss. Paradise is all about him as it was when he was a child, but though he sees it with gladness he does not belong to it. The first four stanzas hold this experience with a peculiarly poignant sense of the longing to share what can no longer be shared. He sees and hears the paradisaical life going on in earth and heaven and among earth's young creatures (there are names for none but the young there, animal or human); but each invitation, in successive stanzas, to be a part of this life, is stopped by sudden sad intrusion of knowledge that it is not any longer his life. The quality of the paradisaical life has an intensely imaginative relevance to the whole poem. It has first of all and last of all the nature of a more than earthly dream; all the common things of Earth are alive with celestial radiance and may be said to be dreaming their own existence in God; it is this that the image of Paradise starts with and (at the end of stanza IV) ends with. In between this beginning and ending the liveliness of this world is imagined. This liveliness shows itself in three special inter-related modes: unity and responsiveness; constant renewal and freshness; the spirit of festival and holy-day. All created things, all creatures, are children of Joy; they respond to each other and to the music of the created harmony of earth and heaven. Not only the birds sing and the lambs bound to this music and the child leaps in his mother's arms, but the moon looks with delight at the festival of life, and the heavens laugh with all blessed creatures at their jubilee; moreover, the rainbow seems obedient to this dance, coming and going; and the cataracts join in unison with their trumpets, while the mountains in their turn throng with the echoes, while the winds bring with them their transcendental freshness. All keep this holy-day, calling and recalling each other, celebrating the fresh renewal of life; all flowers are emblems of this plenitude; and the renewing Sun has every day its glorious birthday.

The imaginative fulness of this paradisaical world is all the more poignantly there because the mature mind hovers for ever about it in longing and cannot enter its dream, feeling the fulness of *its* bliss, but not the fulness of his own. This opening section of the poem is so exactly right because it sustains the vision at the level of myth, while being full of the images of actual life. This world is the world of invisible childhood, not of visible childhood. It is a vision of the unity of all life in the joy of its existence. Erich Neumann, speaking of Chagall, has said: 'For what is childhood but the time of great events; the time in which the great figures are close at hand and look out from behind the corner of the house next door; the time in which the deepest symbols of the soul are everyday realities, and the world is still radiant with its innermost depth? This childhood reaches back to the earliest prehistory and embraces Abraham's angels as tenderly as the neighbour's ass. In this childhood there is as yet no separation between personal and supra-personal, near and far, inward soul and outward world; the life stream flows undivided, joining godhead and man, animal and world, in the glow and colour of the nearby. This simultaneity of inside and outside, which perceives the world in the soul and the soul in the world; this simultaneity of past and future which experiences the promise of the future in the remote past . . .—this is the reality of Chagall's childhood, and the eternal presence of the primordial images lives in his memory. . . .'[5]

Marc Chagall, like Wordsworth, is a man who as a mature artist felt compelled to speak to us through the mask of the child. It is really irrelevant to determine how conscious were artists, like Chagall and Wordsworth, of the immortal childhood they knew as children when they were children. The essence of the childhood described so vividly by Erich Neumann is surely its completely unselfconscious identity with the totality of life. What is important is that this childhood became a peremptory presence in their minds as mature artists, a presence 'not to be put by' and one which they felt to be source of their deepest insights. For Wordsworth, as for Chagall, 'the eternal presence of the primordial images lived in his memory'.

Wordsworth's Ode had rightly to start from this point. The intimations of immortality begin with our first experience of the timeless world, not as a transcendence or escape, but as the real world transfigured, the world in which 'the deepest symbols of the soul are everyday realities'. But none can remain in this first world, for it is a function of our innocence of human life, a function of that unembarrassed, unresisted

[5] Erich Neumann, *Art and the Creative Unconscious*, London, 1959, p. 138.

openness through which the fountain of universal liveliness can play, before any need has arisen to cover, protect, and insulate the anxious ego. We cannot remain in our first world, nor do we wish to. The deepest paradox of all, revealed so dramatically in the Ode, is that the wisdom of life compels the child away from his beatitude of innocence to reach a more difficult and fuller beatitude if he can. The man, in this first part of the poem, who mourns that he is excluded from the eternal spring festival of childhood, excluded himself, not by being betrayed, but willingly, eagerly (as the VIIth stanza reveals), and the more willingly the more creative and active his life. The child turning away from the effortless unity of being into which he was born, turns away out of courage, not his own, but life's; for he must undertake the folly and confusion and violence of human existence as well as its ecstasy, not to be subdued by them, but to bring them into unity, more difficult, more encompassing, than anything the child knows. God, we might say, deliberately pushes man out of Eden, in order that man may work upon the formless chaos outside, and bring it back, if he can, into this garden, redeemed.

The greatness of this poem is that, with an Ode's proper fulness of recognition, it celebrates the central bewildering episode of the story of mankind—that episode which is part of the biological history of man, which is re-enacted in every individual life as it grows to maturity, and which is an allegory of innumerable moments of illumination or obscurity throughout our adult lives.

The poem gathers together first our archetypal childhood, the myth of life still fresh, still in total unity with the Universe, still unburdened with the perplexity of inside and outside, effortlessly in the 'I–thou' relation with all that is, still conscious only of the Dance, not of the I-dancing; and the image of childhood is given with such delicate balance between the language of myth and the language of objective fact, that the mature mind, dandling the dream, knowing its exclusion from it, crying the age-old cry of 'there *was* a time', feels how the dream might at any moment re-assume the actual and return him to the bliss he has lost. But neither mankind nor individual man can turn back down the winding path already travelled. Though his archetype stays within his mind, it is the image of a home, a heaven, a glory, to be perpetually rediscovered in another way by resolutely going on. We must undertake the common life of man, his perplexing imprisonment in the conscious egotistic struggle for mastery, for place, comforted as best we can by the endlessly active goings-on of our earth. We look at children to find them practising their adult lives-to-be, never content to remain in their heaven-born freedom. Only when we have taken on ourselves the yoke of common human existence do we know how to name the radiant vision of childhood. And we are blessed if, in our 'little puddle of light thrown by the gig-lamps of custom' we remember the feel of the immense supernatural vision that childhood knows even   metimes with a tremor of fear; for it is this insight that all creative minds are toiling all their lives to rediscover, not with the shallow innocence of a child, but with the passion, knowledge, and love that is possible to a mature mind.

From *Wordsworth and the Artist's Vision*, University of London, The Athlone Press, 1966, pp. 104–17.

STEPHEN PRICKETT

Wordsworth's Un-Coleridgean Imagination

In Wordsworth the power of poetic creation seems almost always to well up from within him, whereas in Coleridge it seems usually to come from establishing a rapport with the external world—through recognizing a kinship with other creatures, or from the rising wind in the aeolian harp.

We must frame this distinction with some care. Often it would seem to be Wordsworth who has this rapport rather than Coleridge. If we take, for instance, Wordsworth's 'Daffodils' we can see how his sense of dislocation and loneliness is healed by his vision of the daffodils in the wind on the shore of Ullswater. The movement in Wordsworth's description is from, at first sight, a 'fluttering crowd', to a perception of order and harmony as 'a dancing host'.[1] The value of the daffodils lies purely in the didactic function Wordsworth has given them. It is the familiar process of abstracting a moral from nature for later contemplation as a memory. The flowers are merely, in this sense, an anodyne against depression. Wordsworth is not, it seems to me, recognizing any innate kinship between himself and the daffodils in the way that the Ancient Mariner does in the water-snakes.

The choice that seems to have faced both Wordsworth and Coleridge at a certain stage of their development was a moral one—whose outcome was to affect the whole structure of their imaginative development. In the case of Wordsworth, the difficulty of finding out how exactly he did come to envisage the Imagination is considerably aggravated by his ambivalent position between two epochs of thought. His criticism, even when it appears to be echoing Coleridge's, retains always an oddly eighteenth-century flavour—in particular of what Lovejoy has called 'Uniformitarianism': the belief behind his theory of poetry and poetic diction that men everywhere are really very much alike, and that one can, therefore, appeal to the educated for a common consensus of informed opinion. In contrast, as we have seen, his poetry reveals a much sharper and more highly developed power of discrimination. In his Preface to the poems of 1815, for example, he still seems to be thinking of the Imagination as an agent for modifying images by comparisons:

These processes of imagination are carried on either by conferring additional properties upon an object, or abstracting from it those which

[1] Durrant, 'Imagination and Life—Wordsworth's "The Daffodils" ', *Theoria*.

it actually possesses, and thus enabling it to re-act upon the mind which hath performed the process, like a new existence.[2]

As an example of what he means by this, he goes on to cite the description of the Leech-gatherer:

As a huge stone is sometimes seen to lie
Couched on the bald top of an eminence,
Wonder to all who do the same espy
By what means it could thither come, and whence,
So that it seems a thing endued with sense,
Like a sea-beast crawled forth, which on a shelf
Of rock or sand reposeth, there to sun himself.
Such seemed this Man; not all alive or dead
Nor all asleep, in his extreme old age.

Wordsworth explains what is happening in this stanza as follows:

In these images, the conferring, the abstracting, and the modifying powers of the Imagination, immediately and mediately acting, are all brought into conjunction. The stone is endowed with something of the power of life to approximate it to the sea-beast; and the sea-beast stripped of some of its vital qualities to assimilate it to the stone; which intermediate image is thus treated for the purpose of bringing the original image, that of the stone, to a nearer resemblance to the figure and condition of the aged Man; who is divested of so much of the indications of life and motion as to bring him to the point where the two objects unite and coalesce in just comparison.[3]

Elsewhere, this would be interesting; here, what staggers the reader is the way in which Wordsworth has narrowed down the Imagination to a technique of image-formation. He has completely sidestepped the main question of the imaginative structure of the poem—of which the formation of images is an organic part—and is being, in the case of 'Resolution and Independence', less than fair to himself: as we shall see in a moment. More than a decade before this Preface was written, we have seen how Wordsworth's Imagination in the 'Immortality Ode' had taken over the much more radical and architectural role of reorganizing the whole perspective of his memory. It is in this stark discrepancy between poetic practice and theory that Coleridge's criticism of Wordsworth begins. It is against the background of this description of the Imagination by Wordsworth that Coleridge, two years later in *Biographia Literaria*, reacts by trying to describe his Imagination simultaneously as a fact of physics, a psychological process, *and* a metaphysical phenomenon.

The first hint of trouble between them comes almost immediately

[2] *Wordsworth's Literary Criticism*, ed. N. C. Smith (Oxford, 1905), p. 159.
[3] *Ibid.*

after the poetic dialogue to which we have been referring. On 26 October
1803 Coleridge recorded in his notebook:

A most unpleasant Dispute with W. & Hazlitt Wednesday afternoon
. . .—I spoke, I fear too contemptuously—but they spoke so irrever-
ently so malignantly of the Divine Wisdom, that it overset me.
Hazlitt how easily roused to Rage & Hatred, self-projected/but who
shall find the Force that can drag him up out of the Depth into one
expression of Kindness—into the shewing of one Gleam of the Light
of Love on his Countenance—Peace be with *him*!—But *thou*, dearest
Wordsworth—and what if Ray, Durham, Paley, have carried the
observation of the aptitudes of Things too far, too habitually—into
Pedantry?—O how many worse Pedantries! how few so harmless with
so much efficient Good!—Dear William, pardon Pedantry in others &
avoid it in yourself, instead of scoffing & Reviling at Pedantry in good
men in a good cause & *becoming* a Pedant yourself in a bad cause—
even by that very act becoming one!—But surely to look at the superficies of Objects for the purpose of taking Delight in their Beauty, &
sympathy with their real or imagined Life, is as deleterious to the
Health & manhood of Intellect, as always to be peering & unravelling
Contrivances may be to the simplicity of the affections, the grandeur
& unity of the Imagination.—O dearest William! Would Ray, or
Durham, have spoken of God as you spoke of Nature?[4]

It is not easy to see precisely what this dispute, with its accusation,
and counter-accusations of pedantry, was about from this note. Clearly
the division which Coleridge felt so deeply was over an attitude to nature
in Wordsworth that, if allowed unchecked, could (his friend suspected)
permanently damage the whole structure of his imaginative perception
of the world, and consequently his poetry. What, then, did this 'pedantry' consist in? Wordsworth, Coleridge suggests, wishes to look at
the 'superficies of objects' for the express purpose of delighting in their
beauty, and reading into them a pathetic fallacy, and dislikes 'peering
and unravelling Contrivances', which are inimical to the 'grandeur and
unity of the Imagination'. Coleridge, it seems, is arguing that Wordsworth is attempting to apply too rigid a moral utilitarianism to nature.
One thinks again of Wordsworth in 'The Daffodils'. He is less con-

---

[4] *Anima Poetae*, p. 35. The books referred to are Ray's *Wisdom of God in the
Creation*, Paley's *Evidences* and *Natural Theology*, and (if we are to accept
Kathleen Coburn's emendation of 'Durham' to 'Derham') Derham's *Physico-
Theology*. All are orthodox eighteenth-century arguments for the existence of
God from the evidence of 'Design' in nature. What is strange is that Wordsworth seems here to be *attacking* 'evidences of God' while Coleridge is *defending*
them—apparently a complete reversal of their later positions. Coleridge, at this
stage, is clearly willing to entertain the possibility of a 'natural theology' to be
found by man in nature, whereas Wordsworth, as always, seems only really
interested in nature as a subjective extension of his own mind. Ironically, by
the 1820s they appear to have almost exactly reversed positions, each following
still the characteristic needs that began this argument in 1803.

cerned to feel his inter-dependence with nature than he is to find in it an immediate value, or 'message' for him. The 'sermons in stones' may be, as we have seen, very much more than the 'trite reflections of morality' that he turns aside from in Book XI of *The Prelude*, but they are essentially of the same kind: it seems to me here that it is his whole attempt to *use* nature as therapy—the very element that appealed so strongly to John Stuart Mill—that is being so sharply criticized by Coleridge.

We may perhaps see better what I believe Coleridge means about his friend if we look at the way the two poets react to nature in the group of poems under discussion. There is, for instance, in the 'Immortality Ode' very little detailed observation of nature. It is not Wordsworth's response, but his lack of it, that is the central experience. When Coleridge comes, in 'Dejection', to reply to Wordsworth's statement of the sense of loss that afflicts them both ('There was a time when . . .') the difference is immediately felt. Where Wordsworth starts with a generalization about the past, Coleridge begins by way of a most detailed description of the present:

> Well! If the Bard was weather-wise, who made
> The grand old Ballad of Sir Patrick Spence,
> This night, so tranquil now, will not go hence
> Unroused by winds, that ply a busier trade
> Than those which mould yon cloud in lazy flakes . . .

He is giving his poem a specific local setting in time and place. It is the evening of 4 April 1802, and there is a storm brewing. By the first line we have picked up his ruminative and allusive mood. Coleridge is not trying to read into nature a particular message, but rather to establish a rapport with it *as it is*. Almost casually, he uses the schemata of the storm-signs from the 'The Ballad of Sir Patrick Spens' to 'read' the weather, and in doing so suggests a parallel between it, and the way his own mind is already imperceptibly moving. While his own mood follows the course of the storm to its climax, before dying away to a new serenity, Coleridge does not make any real attempt to project his own feelings into the storm—the deliberate projective fantasy of the storm's din in Stanza VII, first as a battle, and then as a little child lost, emphasizes by contrast how much the poem as a whole eschews the pathetic fallacy. What Coleridge wants from the storm is not a 'message' but a sympathetic revival of his own creative Imagination:

> Those sounds which oft have raised me, whilst they awed,
> And sent my soul abroad,
> Might now perhaps their wonted impulse give,
> Might startle this dull pain, and make it move and live!

Hugh Sykes Davies has pointed out how the word 'impulse' is used consistently by Wordsworth in a sense analogous to that of the seven-

teenth-century philosophers. For Wordsworth, he writes, 'it meant not
an inexplicable eddy *within* the human spirit, but a movement stirred in
it from *without*, as an influence upon the individual of some force in the
outer universe'.[5] The only context where Coleridge uses the word in
this sense is here, in 'Dejection'. This was something Coleridge had
learnt from Wordsworth: it is yet another facet of the interplay between
man and nature, and between man and man, for which Coleridge was
constantly seeking new and more satisfactory images. What is so
striking, is that in 'Dejection' there is already a sense in which he has
learnt from Wordsworth, and gone beyond him, to a point where
Wordsworth would not, or could not follow him—to receive the light
reflected as a light bestowed. The immediate result is curious: in spite of
a much deeper pessimism, Coleridge's realization of the present in
contrast to the past is so much firmer than Wordsworth's in the 'Ode'
that it is at once clear that the loss he is complaining of is *not* one of
visual perception:

> I see them all so excellently fair,
> I see, not feel, how beautiful they are.

Coleridge is here putting his finger on the precise difference between
himself and his friend. Wordsworth had written in the 'Ode':

> My heart is at your festival,
> My head hath its coronal,
> The fulness of your bliss, I feel—I feel it all . . .

What Wordsworth felt was threatened was not 'feeling', or sight, but
the 'visionary gleam': a sense of *meaning* in its most literal form. His
philosophic recovery is marked by his new ability to find thoughts 'too
deep for tears' in the meanest flower. Coleridge, on the other hand,
never looked for *thoughts* in nature. He felt his whole imaginative
intercourse with the created world—his whole capacity for open
response—to be threatened, and it is *this* threat that drives him further
into the problem of Imagination and value.

> I may not hope from outward forms to win
> The passion and the life, whose fountains are within.

In the response Coleridge is talking about there is no contradiction
between laborious re-working and spontaneity. In the poem to Wordsworth on first hearing *The Prelude* the image of the breaking wave:

> My soul lay passive, by thy various strain
> Driven as in surges now beneath the stars,
> With momentary stars of my own birth,
> Fair constellated foam, still darting off
> Into the darkness . . .

[5] 'Wordsworth and the Empirical Philosophers', *The English Mind*, ed.
Watson (Cambridge, 1964), p. 155.

is taken, almost to the word, from Satyrane's First Letter, published first in *The Friend*, and then in *Biographia Literaria*.[6]

A beautiful white cloud of Foam at momentary intervals coursed by the side of the Vessel with a Roar, and little stars of flame danced and sparkled and went out in it: and every now and then light detachments of this white cloud-like foam dashed off from the vessel's side, each with its own small constellation, over the sea, and scoured out of sight like a Tartar Troop over a wilderness.

Clearly, whatever Coleridge meant by 'Pedantry', he did not refer it to the construction of perceptions. It is not merely that he is taking as an image for his feeling the memory of a particular observation of foam at sea, but he is harking back verbally to a previous literary schema. Coleridge's 'spontaneous' response can immediately be analysed in terms of 'making and matching'.

Simultaneously, we have a glimpse of the enormous importance that he attaches to detailed observation. His notebooks and poems alike are full of the most minutely detailed descriptions of nature.[7] Few comparisons are more symptomatic of this difference between Wordsworth and Coleridge than the contrast between this sense of 'inscape' in 'Dejection' and the way Wordsworth opens 'Resolution and Independence':

There was a roaring in the wind all night;
The rain came heavily and fell in floods;
But now the sun is rising calm and bright;
The birds are singing in the distant woods:
Over his own sweet voice the stock-dove broods;
The jay makes answer as the magpie chatters;
And all the air is filled with pleasant noise of waters.

It is the morning after the storm; a symbolic sequel to the storm that had raged for Coleridge in 'Dejection'. But the effect is as deliberately diffused and generalized as Coleridge's was intense and particular. It could be any morning after any storm, for Wordsworth (for all his dislike of Johnson as a critic) is answering Coleridge's individual problem with a general truth. The jays and the stock-dove are named, but only as sound-effects to the prevailing mood. One bird stands for the species. In the next stanza we encounter the hare:

All things that love the sun are out of doors:
The sky rejoices in the morning's birth;
The grass is bright with rain-drops;—on the moors
The hare is running races in her mirth;

[6] See note by E. H. Coleridge, *Poems of S.T.C.*, p. 408.

[7] Humphry House (*Coleridge*: Clark Lectures, 1951–2 (Hart-Davies, 1953)) notes the similarity between Coleridge and Gerard Manley Hopkins in a number of places, and advances the suggestion that Hopkins may have had access to the *Notebooks* during his Oxford friendship with E. H. Coleridge.

And with her feet she from the plashy earth
Raises a mist; that, glittering in the sun,
Runs with her all the way, wherever she doth run.

So vivid is the description that we are not immediately aware of its ambiguity: is this, like the stock-dove, one hare standing for many, or is this one particular hare? Is it, in other words, an exquisitely realized detail of the landscape of the mind brought momentarily into focus as an example of the joyous resurgence of nature after the storm, or is it a solitary individual, a counterpart to the solitary poet himself, or the aged Leech-gather, to be contrasted with his environment? The animal, as an unthinking child of nature, is drawing clouds of glory from the earth at every bound; can the poet do the same, or is he (after the experience of the 'Immortality Ode') separated by the mystery of human growth from this unreflecting abandoned joy? In the next stanza the ambiguity is resolved at the level of the narrative: evidently it is now an individual hare—but the gulf between the general and the particular has been spanned rhetorically, and the tension between unity and dissent has already been subliminally suggested. The way for Wordsworth's own polarity of mood has now been prepared:

But, as it sometimes chanceth, from the sight
Of joy in minds that can no farther go,
As high as we have mounted in delight
In our dejection do we sink as low,
To me that morning did it happen so;
And fears, and fancies, thick upon me came;
Dim sadness—and blind thoughts, I knew not, nor could name.

As in the 'Immortality Ode', the scene of apparent pastoral bliss hides a deeply disturbing note. The movement of the poem is towards a discrimination and clarification of what causes this disturbance. Wordsworth shifts our attention from the outside world to his own inner world, echoing Coleridge's own desperate discovery in 'Dejection':

By our own spirits are we deified:
We poets in our youth begin in gladness;
But thereof comes in the end despondency and madness.

The self-sufficiency of this 'deification'—both like, and unlike Coleridge's 'glory, enveloping the earth'—is ominous, perhaps, but does not warrant the latter's charge of 'pedantry'. Nature and the mind are unified, in poetry as in perception, by an imaginative act that finds an answering resonance in moors and waters to the tensions of the poet.

But it seems to me that at this point the poem falls into two. Wordsworth is rescued from his dilemma by outside intervention of a peculiarly ambiguous kind:

Now, whether it were by peculiar grace,
A leading from above, a something given,

Yet it befel, that, in this lonely place,
When I with these untoward thoughts had striven,
Beside a pool bare to the eye of heaven
I saw a man before me unawares . . .

There is a visionary and supernatural quality to the aged Leech-gatherer
that marks him off from the world of the stock-dove. What overwhelms
Wordsworth about him is a feeling of *intervention* in the natural order:

the whole body of the man did seem
Like one whom I had met with in a dream;
Or like a man from some far region sent,
To give me human strength, by apt admonishment.

Simultaneously, something dramatic has happened to the natural
scenery. The sunshine and the woods have vanished. In their place is a
world of 'bare pools' in lonesome places on the 'weary moors'. This is the
scenery of the visionary dreariness of *The Prelude*; scenery that we have
learned, paradoxically, to associate with the restoration of the Imagination. There is, of course, a simple naturalistic explanation for all this:
Wordsworth has left the lush lakeland valley and climbed up on to the
bare and peaty shoulder of the fells. But even in this there is a topo-
graphical symbolism. Moses-like, the poet has climbed from the world
of the senses to the austerity of the naked spirit. Yet there is still another
side to this abrupt climatic change. Wordsworth was initially at one with
nature. Then, in the midst of harmony, came doubts and perplexities.
Now, with the strange, almost supernatural meeting with the Leech-
gatherer, he encounters an image of resolute opposition to a hostile
environment. If Wordsworth is to emulate the heroism of the Leech-
gatherer he so much admires, he must take up employment 'hazardous
and wearisome' fighting inhospitable desolation for ever-diminishing
returns. The paradox is that it is just this hopeless heroism that seems to
offer him a way through the perplexities that had originally troubled
him:

My former thoughts returned: the fear that kills;
And hope that is unwilling to be fed;
Cold, pain, and labour, and all fleshly ills;
And mighty poets in their misery dead.
Perplexed, and longing to be comforted
My question eagerly did I renew . . .

But what was 'perplexing' Wordsworth was a quite specific worry: his
possible poetic decline. What if his 'summer mood' were to end?
Chatterton, 'the marvellous boy' had died young; Burns, 'he who
followed the plough', was a peasant primitive whose development was
no guide to Wordsworth's own; and—the unspoken fear—Coleridge,
the one poet against whom Wordsworth could measure himself, had
written 'Dejection':

. . . thereof comes in the end despondency and madness.

I do not think we can understand why the hopeless heroic stoicism of the old Leech-gatherer seemed so attractive to Wordsworth unless we can first see why he felt he *must* reject his previous openness and receptivity to nature. His answer—and it is hard to read it as *not* addressed to Coleridge—seems to be: 'That way lies madness!' The other alternative —which we must more and more identify with Coleridge—that of struggling at an ever-increasing cost to assert kinship with the created world, was, for Wordsworth, an even more terrifying prospect. The Leech-gatherer's magnificent resolution was for him the lesser of the two evils.

> and when he ended,
> I could have laughed myself to scorn to find
> In that decrepit man so firm a mind.
> 'God,' said I, 'be my help and stay secure;
> I'll think of the leech-gatherer on the lonely moor!'

What is noticeable to us is that in making this choice there has already been a distinct hardening of sensibility. The message now is one of struggle, not of understanding. To that extent he has already left behind the world of the 'Immortality Ode':

> To me the meanest flower that blows can give
> Thoughts that do often lie too deep for tears.

Instead the painful process of gathering an ever-declining number of leeches is certainly a very ambiguous image of poetic creation. We are reminded irresistibly of Coleridge's charge of pedantry, endangering 'manhood of intellect' by using nature to satisfy emotional needs, rather than responding to it. If Wordsworth is really throwing in his lot with the Leech-gatherer, then surely Coleridge is right. Wordsworth's own definition of 'Imagination' in his Preface of 1815, and his choice of examples from 'Resolution and Independence' which we have already looked at, suggest a logical continuation of his attempt to build a poetic structure that would tame and didacticize nature without correspondingly modifying the creating mind of the poet.

Coleridge's reference to 'pedantry' in his friend's attitude to nature dates from 1803. It is, I suspect, a part of the tension between them that was at first to prove so creative, and finally, so destructive. The poetic dialogue we have been examining continued spasmodically from 1800 until Coleridge's poem to Wordsworth on the completion of *The Prelude* in 1807. It spans in time, and is largely responsible for much of their best work. Each seemed capable during these years of providing the other with schemata to react against, and to work from.

From *Coleridge and Wordsworth: The Poetry of Growth*, Cambridge: The University Press, 1970, pp. 156–67.

Select Bibliography

TEXTS:

EDITIONS:

Lyrical Ballads, edited by R. L. Brett and A. R. Jones, London: Methuen, 1963.

The Poetical Works of William Wordsworth, 5 vols, edited by Ernest de Selincourt and Helen Darbishire, Oxford: Clarendon Press, 1940–1949.

The Prelude, edited by Ernest de Selincourt; revised by Helen Darbishire, Oxford: Clarendon Press, 1959.

Prose Works of William Wordsworth, 3 vols, edited by A. B. Grosart, London: Moxon, 1876.

The Early Letters of William and Dorothy Wordsworth, 1787–1805, Oxford: Clarendon Press, 1935.

The Letters of William and Dorothy Wordsworth: The Middle Years, 2 vols, Oxford: Clarendon Press, 1937.

The Letters of William and Dorothy Wordsworth: The Later Years, 3 vols, Oxford: Clarendon Press, 1939.

(All six volumes edited by Ernest de Selincourt.)

Second edition of the *Letters:*

The Early Years, revised by Chester L. Shaver, Oxford: Clarendon Press, 1967.

An indispensable guide to Wordsworth's theories and opinions is: Markham L. Peacock, Jr., *The Critical Opinions of William Wordsworth,* Baltimore: John Hopkins, 1950.

BIOGRAPHIES:

George Maclean Harper, *William Wordsworth: His Life, Works, and Influence,* 2 vols, London: Murray, 1916.

Emile Legouis, *The Early Life of William Wordsworth, 1770–1798,* London: Dent, 1897.

Mary Moorman, *William Wordsworth: A Biography. The Early Years, 1770–1803* (1957). *The Later Years, 1803–1850* (1965), Oxford: Clarendon Press.

CRITICAL STUDIES (TWENTIETH CENTURY):

BOOKS:

Lascelles Abercrombie, *The Art of Wordsworth,* London: Oxford University Press, 1952.

M. H. Abrams, *Natural Supernaturalism: Tradition and Revolution in Romantic Literature,* London: Oxford University Press, 1971.

F. W. Bateson, *Wordsworth: A Re-Interpretation,* London: Longmans, 1954.

Edith C. Batho, *The Later Wordsworth*, Cambridge: University Press, 1933.

Arthur Beatty, *William Wordsworth: His Doctrine and Art in Their Historical Relations*, Madison: University Press, 1922.

Mary Burton, *The One Wordsworth*, Chapel Hill: University of North Carolina Press, 1942.

Colin Clarke, *Romantic Paradox*, London: Routledge and Kegan Paul, 1962.

John F. Danby, *The Simple Wordsworth*, London: Routledge and Kegan Paul, 1960.

Helen Darbishire, *The Poet Wordsworth*, Oxford: Clarendon Press, 1950.

Hugh I'A. Fausset, *The Lost Leader*, London: Jonathan Cape, 1933.

David Ferry, *The Limits of Mortality*, Middletown, Connecticut: Wesleyan University Press, 1959.

H. W. Garrod, *Wordsworth*, Oxford: Clarendon Press, 1927.

Geoffrey H. Hartman, *Wordsworth Poetry, 1787–1814*, New Haven and London: Yale University Press, 1964.

R. D. Havens, *The Mind of a Poet: A Study of Wordsworth's Thought with Particular Reference to 'The Prelude'*, Baltimore: John Hopkins, 1941.

James A. W. Heffernan, *Wordsworth Theory of Poetry. The Transforming Imagination*, Ithaca and London: Cornell University Press, 1969.

C. H. Herford, *Wordsworth*, London: Routledge, 1930.

John Jones, *The Egotistical Sublime*, London: Chatto and Windus, 1954.

Alec King, *Wordsworth and the Artist's Vision*, University of London: The Athlone Press, 1966.

J. S. Lyon, *The Excursion: A Study*, New Haven: Yale University Press, 1950.

Kenneth MacLean, *Agrarian Age: A Background for Wordsworth*, New Haven: Yale University Press, 1950.

Florence Marsh, *Wordsworth's Imagery*, New Haven: Yale University Press, 1952.

H. M. Margoliouth, *Wordsworth and Coleridge, 1795–1834*, London: Oxford University Press, 1953.

Roger N. Murray, *Wordsworth's Style. Figures and Themes in the 'Lyrical Ballads' of 1800*, Lincoln: University of Nebraska Press, 1967.

H. W. Piper, *The Active Universe*, London: Athlone Press, 1962. (Two chapters specifically on Wordsworth.)

Stephen Prickett, *Wordsworth and Coleridge: The Poetry of Growth*, London: Routledge and Kegan Paul, 1970.

Abbie F. Potts, *Wordsworth's Prelude: A Study of its Literary Form*, Ithaca: Cornell University Press, 1953.

Melvin Rader, *Wordsworth: A Philosophical Approach*, Oxford: Clarendon Press, 1967.

Walter Raleigh, *Wordsworth*, London: Edward Arnold, 1903.

Herbert Read, *Wordsworth*, London: Cape, 1930.

W. L. Sperry, *Wordsworth's Anti-Climax*, Cambridge: Harvard University Press, 1935.

Newton P. Stallknecht, *Strange Seas of Thought: Studies in William Wordsworth's Philosophy of Man and Nature*, Bloomington and London: Indiana University Press, 1966.

F. M. Todd, *Politics and the Poet: A Study of Wordsworth*, London: Methuen, 1957.

Enid Welsford, *Salisbury Plain. A Study in the Development of Wordsworth's Mind and Art*, Oxford: Blackwell, 1966.

Jonathan Wordsworth, *The Music of Humanity*, London: Nelson, 1969.

ESSAYS:

M. H. Abrams, 'Wordsworth and the Eighteenth Century', *The Mirror and the Lamp: Romantic Theory and the Critical Tradition*, New York: Norton, 1958, pp. 103–14.

Bernard Blackstone, 'The Secondary Founts', *The Lost Travellers*, London: Longmans, 1962, pp. 90–139.

Harold Bloom, 'William Wordsworth', *The Visionary Company*, London: Faber, pp. 120–93.

A. C. Bradley, 'Wordsworth', *Oxford Lectures on Poetry*, London: Macmillan, 1909, pp. 99–148.

Donald Davie, 'Syntax in the Blank Verse of Wordsworth's "Prelude"', *Articulate Energy: An Enquiry into the Syntax of English Verse*, London: Routledge and Kegan Paul, pp. 106–16.

Salvador de Madariaga, 'The Case of Wordsworth', *Shelley and Calderon*, London: Constable, 1920, pp. 126–90.

T. S. Eliot, 'Wordsworth and Coleridge', *The Use of Poetry and the Use of Criticism*, London: Faber and Faber, 1933, pp. 67–85.

William Empson, 'Sense in "The Prelude" ', *The Structure of Complex Words*, London: Chatto and Windus, 1951, pp. 289–305.

D. W. Harding, 'Concrete Embodiment: Emblem and Symbol', *Experience into Words*, London: Chatto and Windus, 1963, pp. 72–90.

John O. Hayden,' Wordsworth', *The Romantic Reviewers: 1802–1824* London: Routledge and Kegan Paul, 1969, pp. 78–103.

G. Wilson Knight, 'The Wordsworthian Profundity', *The Starlit Dome*, London: Oxford University Press, 1941, pp. 1–82.

F. R. Leavis, 'Wordsworth', *Revaluation*, London: Chatto and Windus, pp. 154–202.

Lionel Trilling, 'The Immortality Ode', *The Liberal Imagination*, London: Mercury, 1961 (first published 1951), pp. 129–59.

Basil Willey, 'On Wordsworth and the Locke Tradition', *The Seventeenth Century Background*, London: Chatto and Windus, 1950, pp. 296–309.

ARTICLES:

Edward E. Bostetter, 'Wordsworth's Dim and Perilous Way', *P.M.L.A.*, LXXXI, 1956, pp. 433–50.

Patrick Cruttwell, 'Wordsworth, the Public and the People', *Sewanee Review*, LXIV, 1956, pp. 71–80.

Barbara Everett, '"The Prelude"', *The Critical Quarterly*, I, 1959, pp. 338–50.

Albert S. Gérard, 'Dark Passages: Exploring "Tintern Abbey"', *Studies in Romanticism*, III, 1963, pp. 1–23.

Robert Mayo, 'The Contemporaneity of the "Lyrical Ballads"', *P.M.L.A.*, LXIX, 1954, pp. 486–522.

Josephine Miles, 'Wordsworth and Glitter', *Studies in Philology*, XL, 1943, pp. 552–59.

Edwin Morgan, 'A Prelude to *The Prelude*', *Essays in Criticism*, V, 1955, pp. 341–53.

T. M. Raysor, 'The Establishment of Wordsworth's Reputation', *Journal of English and Germanic Philology*, LIV, 1955, pp. 61–71.

Christopher Ricks, 'A Pure Organic Pleasure from the Lines', *Essays in Criticism*, XXI, 1971, pp. 1–29.

Roger Sharrock, 'Wordsworth's Revolt against Literature', *Essays in Criticism*, III, 1953, pp. 396–412.

James Smith, 'Wordsworth: A Preliminary Survey', *Scrutiny*, VII, 1938, pp. 33–5.

GUIDES TO CONTEMPORARY CRITICISM (1789–1850):

Elsie Smith (ed.), *An Estimate of William Wordsworth by his Contemporaries, 1793–1822*, Oxford: Blackwell, 1932.

John Wain (ed.), *Contemporary Reviews of Romantic Poetry*, London: Harrap, 1953.

GUIDES TO SUBSEQUENT CRITICISM:

Patricia Hodgart and Theodore Redpath, *Romantic Perspectives*, London: Harrap, 1964.

James V. Logan, *Wordsworthian Criticism: A Guide and Bibliography*, Columbus: Ohio State University Press, 1947.

Muriel Spark and Derek Stanford, *Tribute to Wordsworth*, London: Wingate, 1950.

ANTHOLOGIES OF MODERN CRITICISM:

J. Davies (ed.), *Discussions of Wordsworth*, London: Heath, 1964.

A. W. Thompson (ed.), *Wordsworth's Mind and Art*, Edinburgh: Oliver and Boyd, 1969.